THE

HEADLESS

WOMAN

by Bob Layton

Contents

FOREWORD

THIS STORY, PARTLY BIOGRAPHICAL BUT fictionalized to fit the time-line, is set in a small town in the late 1950s. It's the story of how many adventures boys can have with their BB guns. Some end with rewards, others with regrets. It's also the story of how a failing church food booth at the fair found success through a carnival-type illusion called The Headless Woman, and how the "BB boys" made that happen.

As children, we parroted much of what we heard the adults say, seldom questioning the status quo. And so it was, that the gentleman who ran the corner store that would be an eventual predecessor to the 7-11 and many others, was largely referred to in many communities, simply as "the Chinaman."

We knew nothing much about the man. We did not know how he came to be in our town, and for the merchant who lived by himself, it never crossed our young minds how lonely he might be.

I owe a huge debt of gratitude to Melvin Wong. Like me, he was a child in the same era, and his parents ran a Chinese Restaurant called *Delicious,* in a town not far from where I grew up. He was a huge part of helping me see the point of view of the Chinese merchants at that time. I hope I have shown them the proper respect.

CHAPTER ONE

WHO WOULD HAVE THOUGHT THIS day would end with me telling a child about a boy with a pair of scissors sticking out of his forehead?

Scissors. Let's see. How would you say that in Mandarin? I'll have to check in my English to Chinese Dictionary. So far I can count to ten verbally and carefully offer a greeting. I had been taking an evening course in Mandarin, until it was cancelled by Covid-19. The last class had us singing "Heads, shoulders, knees and toes…"

My daughter, Anne, was interested in how I was doing and I drove to her home to visit for just a few minutes, at least that was my plan. This would be the first place I would be able to walk into today without a mask.

I could hear computer game music before I even opened the front door. I found my grandson Jeremy squatting on the living room floor in front of the T.V., furiously working the controller.

"HI, JEREMY!" I said, loud enough to be heard over the music and wild sound effects.

"Hi, Grandpa," he replied, not looking up as he deftly made a move.

"IS YOUR MOM HOME?"

Without missing a beat, he reached up with a toe and clicked off the stereo. "I didn't know you could get that much volume out of those games," I smiled.

"You can if you plug it through the stereo," he replied. He still did not look up; instead, he nodded as he apparently made a good move.

"So, where's your mom?" I asked.

"In the kitchen," he squeaked. His voice faltered for a moment as he tilted to the right to perform whatever it was he was doing. Anne came in from the kitchen just as Jeremy lost his balance and sprawled on the floor.

"So, what's happening?" asked Anne. I showed her my Chinese finger counting.

Jeremy was curious. "Why are you learning Chinese, Grandpa?"

I explained that with retirement just a few years away, I thought I might like to go see the Great Wall of China. Interpreters were all right, but I wanted some basic idea of what was going on around me.

"It's a shame, you know," I said. "I could have learned Chinese as a boy. There was a fellow I could have asked. I just had no idea I would ever want to learn it. When you get older you start to see the missed opportunities for all kinds of things."

I was about to leave when Anne said to Jeremy, "I'm a little surprised to see you playing games. Haven't you got a first-aid test tonight at Scouts?"

"I'm all ready, Mom."

"So, you think you'll get your first-aid badge?"

"Easy."

"Great. I had *my* first-aid badge..." I started.

"Uh-huh, So you've told me a bunch of times," he replied, a slightly bored look on his face.

2

"I hear your camping trip won't be a Covid problem since it's all basically outside. Any more word on it?"

"Ya." He sounded dejected.

"Something wrong?"

"Ya. It's Mr. Black."

"The new Scoutmaster?"

"Ya. Some of the guys don't like him. They might not go on the camp. I might not go, either."

"What's the problem?"

"Dumb camping rules," said Jeremy.

"Like what?" I asked.

"No tunes and no cell phones and no guns," complained Jeremy.

"Well, Jeremy, you are going out there to learn woodcraft. You can't listen to him if you're wearing earbuds, now can you?" I chuckled.

"He says we can't even bring phones in our tents at night. And, he doesn't want us bringing any of *that* kind of music. That's what he said."

Anne suggested: "Maybe he just doesn't want you to miss out on the music of the woods, Jeremy. The sound of the wind through the trees, the babbling brooks, the call of the wild..."

"Aw, Mom. That's corny!"

"He's pretty well qualified, isn't he, Dad?" Anne asked me.

"Ron Black? You bet. He's a park ranger. We're lucky to have him. What did you say about guns, Jeremy? No one has a gun here in the city, do they?"

"The Barton brothers have .22s. They live on an acreage so they go shooting all the time, but he said they couldn't bring them along because we'll be camping in a National Park."

"Sounds right to me," I said. Anne went back into the kitchen.

"But Jimmie Faraday has a pellet gun and he won't let him bring that, either," I complained

"I'm sure Scouter Black just doesn't want anyone to get hurt, Jeremy," said Anne.

"Aw, Mom, we'd only shoot at targets. Everybody would get a try."

"Still," she said, "there's always the chance of someone getting hurt."

"Or getting into a little mischief," I added, starting to remember days past.

"What are you smiling about?" she asked me. "You've got that *smile*."

"Oh, nothing," I lied, rather wishing I hadn't brought it up.

"When you smile like that, Dad, it's not *nothing*. I can tell when you're thinking something," teased Anne.

"So, will you talk to him about the music, Grandpa?" asked Jeremy. "It's not fair to have someone old tell you not to listen to your music."

"I've *been there*, Jeremy," I said. "I know exactly where you're coming from, but you'll have to live without your music for a whole three days. And I'm afraid I'm going to have to agree with the rule against any kind of guns - even BB guns - as well."

"Aw, Grandpa. How come?"

"I've been there too, Jeremy."

"What do you mean?"

"It looks like you've got time before supper. Why don't you shut off the game and I'll tell you what happened to me when I was your age."

"You won't get it done before supper anyway," called Anne from the kitchen. "Besides, I want to hear this, too."

Jeremy thought for a moment, then pressed the pause button. He turned around and leaned with his back against the end of the couch. He looked up at me, and his eyes said *let's get it over with*.

"Well, Jeremy," I began.

CHAPTER TWO

W^{E COULD SEE HOW THEY} thought it was us who did it, all right; but they were *wrong*. Our guns just weren't that powerful. We told everyone they *were*, but we were lying our faces off. We claimed our guns had been fitted with a special mechanism to make them as powerful as a .22. We did that after a farm boy mocked us for having toys when he had real rifles. Dilly even bragged his was *more* powerful than a .22, but then he had to take it back when he was challenged to take a shot at a license plate on the wall of Harding's Garage.

Now here we were trying to take back the fib, and everyone thought we were lying about Mr. Martin's window, instead.

We were out shooting that afternoon, all right, in Dilly's back yard. Shooting at a bulls-eye target we had taped to the side of his neighbor's garage. It was sided with corrugated steel, so it made lots of noise when we hit the target, but old man Miller was deaf so he didn't know what was going on.

Besides, we were shooting east. Mr. Martin lived south - across the street. Our guns wouldn't shoot all the way from Dilly's back yard, across the street and clear across to Mr. Martin's front yard, and still have the power to pop a hole in his window. They just wouldn't.

We tried to convince our dads of that, but Mr. Martin was making more noise than the three of us put together. All Mr. Martin knew was he came home from work and there was a tiny hole and a crack in his window. He looked closely at it, and could see only the first pane had been damaged. There, lying on the sill between the panes was the copper colored culprit: a single BB.

He wanted to call the cops but our dads didn't want any part of dealing with the police. Instead, they agreed we would pay for the replacement window, so Mr. Martin relaxed a bit. A new window, installed, was going to be about fifty-five dollars. It was just lucky for us that Cally's dad owned the hardware store, and he offered to get the window and have it installed for thirty dollars. Ten bucks each. Thirty bucks for something we didn't do. That hurt. That really hurt. That our dads didn't believe us also added to the pain.

But that discussion was outside in the yard. When I came into the house, things got even worse when my mom heard about it.

"Lester John West," scolded my mother. "I told your father you were not to have a BB gun. I told him there would be trouble. Did he listen to me? Does he ever listen to me?"

"It wasn't us, Mom."

"What if it had been a person who got hit instead of a window? For sure the police would have to be involved."

I had no idea how to answer that.

"And who are those other trouble-makers you were with?"

"They're not trouble-makers."

"Calvin Borstad," she fumed. "Is that Elmer's boy?"

"Elmer and Caroline; yeah, that's their kid," replied Dad.

"And what is it you call the other one? Dilly? Did I hear you boys call him Dilly? Is that his name, Lester?" asked Mom.

"Not really," I answered, trying not to sound too bored with her tirade.

"Well, what is it, *really*?" she demanded.

"Peter," I said, quietly.

"What? Speak up. I can't hear you when you mumble!"

"It's PETER! Peter Brock."

"Peter? So why do they call him Dilly?"

"Because he likes helping his mom make dill pickles. He talks about it every summer. Wants us to come over and see how they do it but we don't care. They've got a cucumber field out by somebody's farm or something. He thinks it's a big deal to make pickles."

"That would be Ella Brock's boy. She brought the pickles to the last church supper. They were very tasty," Mom remembered, licking her lips.

"Whatever," I said.

"*You* don't call him Dilly, do you?" she asked, pointedly.

"Everybody calls him that, Mom."

"Well, you shouldn't. It's not respectful. Time you learned a little respect. You're about to begin high school, after all. The boys call you Lester, don't they?"

"Well, ya..." She didn't have a clue.

"Well then, show them a little respect, too. This Peter and Calvin, have they got money to pay for the window?"

"No, I don't think so."

"And they both have those BB guns?"

"Ya."

"Maybe you boys will have to sell them to raise the money," she suggested.

I shook my head.

"Then what will you do?" she demanded.

"School's out in two more days," I said. "Then there's the rodeo. Then we're going picking beans at Jensen's farm."

"Have you already asked the Jensens? I'd think they'd have enough people by now."

"Yes, we did. They'll be coming into town at five in the morning the day after the rodeo. Everyone who wants to pick beans has to be on the sidewalk in front of the China – uh – uh - Fong's store," he said, as his mother's lips began to purse. "They'll drive us out to the farm."

"What are they paying these days to pick string beans?" Dad asked.

"Two cents a pound."

He drew his breath between his teeth. "It's going to take a lot of beans to pay for that window."

"Which we never broke..." I started.

"Knock it off," warned Dad. "Did you see anyone else in that neighborhood with a BB gun?"

I shook my head.

"Education is expensive, Lester."

"What?"

"If it wasn't you boys, if there's someone else in the neighborhood with a BB gun we don't know about, then you just learned an expensive lesson. You shouldn't be shooting those guns in town. You ought to go biking out in the country somewhere and set up something to shoot at. I thought that's what you'd been doing all this time."

I just nodded. We *had* been going out into the country. We'd spent our allowance on a big package of balloons. We found a tree with lots of low branches on it, and we blew up those balloons and tied them all along the branches. Then we marked off how far we thought the balloon wall was at the fairgrounds last year, and started shooting. This year, we should win a big prize. Easy.

This was, after all, our whole mission. Last year, we used the BB guns they supplied at the fair but did not win anything. This year, we were each going to win. That's why we felt target practice was so important.

Aiming carefully along the tree branch, we broke a few balloons, and then a sparrow landed on the branch. We all stopped shooting and just looked at each other. And smiled. Nobody had to say anything. We knew we were all thinking exactly the same thing. The young soldiers were about to be blooded.

Cally levered another BB into his chamber. Dilly did the same. They both watched as I worked the lever of my gun as quietly as possible. Scaring the bird at this point would be a sacrilege.

We raised our barrels in unison. "I get first shot," whispered Cally. "I saw him first." We didn't believe that, but he called it, so he got it. That was the rule. Cally squeezed the trigger. *Pap.* Then he cursed softly under his breath. He had missed. "Went right by his head. A breeze... probably..." he said, lamely.

"MY shot," announced Dilly, hopefully. He flexed his fingers around the stock, gripping and re-gripping. Then, *pap.* "I got him! I got him!" he shouted gleefully. We ran forward to see our first kill.

The sparrow had been knocked off the branch and was now lying in the tall weeds at the bottom of the tree. The sparrow, however, was not dead. It was struggling. Frantic. Trying desperately to fly but instead just thrashing about. Finally, it lay quivering; we could see the ugly wound in its breast. The little bird was scared. It tried to get up on one tiny leg but fell over. A small, ruined, feather marked the spot where it had fallen. Its tiny eyes were wide as its body convulsed in terror. It was the most horrible thing we had ever seen.

Dilly put his hand over his mouth but it was too late. He was already wretching. Finally, he lost his lunch and the already injured bird suffered the indignity of vomit on its deathbed.

"Kill it!" choked Dilly. "Kill it. Come on, you're still loaded up, Fester. Do it!"

I pointed the muzzle at the little bird's head, and turned my own head away. I took a tense little breath and squeezed the trigger. *Pap.* We stood there for a moment. Brightly colored balloons had done duty at many a birthday party. Now they were the funeral flowers for a dead sparrow.

Dilly turned away, kicking his foot in the dirt. Then he angrily jammed the butt of his rifle into a soft mound and began scooping out a hole.

"What are you doing?" asked Cally.

"Looks like he's digging a little grave," I suggested, quietly.

Dilly didn't answer. After a moment he went over to the still body of the bird and used his foot to push the little corpse over to the little hole. He pushed it in, kicked dirt over it, and then planted his foot right on top to pack it down.

"Let's get the rest of the balloons," suggested Cally, breaking the sombre mood. There were half a dozen left. I got two. He got three. Then we realized Dilly wasn't shooting. He was sitting on the ground, watching us. "Want the last one?" Cally asked him.

"Don't care," Dilly replied.

"Go ahead," offered Cally, but Dilly just shrugged.

"The midway will be here next week, man," I said. "We want to take those guys for some good stuff this year..."

No answer.

"Didn't you want to get those binocs?" Cally prodded. "Come on, we've been waiting a whole year for the carnival to come back.

Dilly stayed sitting in the dirt. With his right leg sideways on the ground, he raised his left knee, tucking his foot in close to his body. He rested his left elbow on his left knee and used it to steady his gun. *Pap.* The balloon exploded.

We had saved the red one for last.

On the way home we agreed to never tell the story of the bird to anyone. Our BB guns would be used only for target practice from now on.

Little did we know what the next few days had in store.

CHAPTER THREE

R EVEREND SCHMIDTKE DELIVERED A SHORTER sermon than usual because he wanted to talk about the rodeo and the fair that began the next morning: in particular, our booth on the midway. There were eight churches in our area, and every church was allowed a tent to sell hot dogs or hamburgers or corn on the cob or soda pop or maybe ice cream. The individual tent locations were chosen every year at the meeting of the Rascal River Ministerial Council, and everyone picked a location out of a hat.

"Bad news," said Reverend Schmidtke apologetically. "We got spot number *eight*." There was an "Oooooo" from the congregation and he held up his hands for silence. "We'll make do," he promised. "With the help of the good Lord, we'll earn the money we need. Let us bow our heads and pray."

I didn't know how bad spot number eight was until we got to the grounds. Our family was in the group that started at noon, and when we arrived we could see it was a very bad location. The best spot was near the grandstand. If people were going to sit down for a couple of hours they liked to eat. After that, people walked along the midway and bought from the food tents among the games of chance. We were right at the end, near the parking area. The games separating us from the rest of the midway looked pretty boring, and the barkers were already busy trying to get people to come and play.

"Just two bits," one shouted. "Look how big the hoops are! If the hoop lassoes the bottle, you win a prize! Who's next? How about winning a teddy bear for the little lady?" he shouted to a passing cowboy and his girl. The cowboy waved him off, but before he got to our tent, he turned and walked back down the midway. We watched as he stopped at one of the other tents for a burger a few stalls down.

One of our members was bored, and he wandered over to the nearby "dime in the dish" game. My dad put his elbows on the counter with his hands at his chest, and rested his chin on his hands. "Watch Zeke throw his money away, Lester."

Sure enough, Zeke tried twice but the dime slipped off the edge of the plate and down among the stuffed animals both times. Zeke came shame-facedly back to the tent with his hands thrust down deep in his pockets.

"They do it with flour," Dad said quietly to me.

"What do you mean, flour?" I asked.

"The plates are coated with flour. They dust it on, and then blow it off. There's just a trace left to make those plates slick as a whistle."

"How do you know that, Dad?" I asked.

"I think I must have read it somewhere," he replied.

Mom put down the onion she was chopping up. "Your father knows all about that, don't you, Hal?"

He smiled a little, and nodded, and then turned away as if he was embarrassed.

"So, how do you know all this, Dad?" I asked.

"Oh, it's a long story. Doesn't really matter."

"Tell him, Hal. Fathers are supposed to teach their sons what they know. Tell him about the carnival."

"Thought you didn't want anybody to know about that," he said softly.

"It's been a long time, Hal. You're not into that nonsense anymore. I think you ought to tell him how things work, before he goes out and wastes his money. Don't you?"

"How what works?" asked Reverend Schmidtke, who had just arrived.

"The carnival," answered Mom. "The games on the midway. Hal traveled with the carnival for a couple of years before he started driving truck. Left the midway after the summer of nineteen forty-seven I think it was. Yes, about ten or eleven years ago." Then, "You were just little, Lester."

"You were a carnie?" asked the Reverend.

"Yeah. Just one of the many things I did after the war."

"What did you do?" he pressed.

"Mostly I worked the bally stand."

"What's a bally stand?" I asked.

"Bally*hoo*, Lester," answered the Reverend. "It's all bally-hoo. Talk up the rubes and get them to part with their money."

"What are rubes?" I asked.

"Local folks," smiled the Reverend.

"You seem to know the lingo," said my dad, suspiciously. "How come?"

"Well," smiled the Reverend, "let's just say I went around the block a couple of times before I started doing God's work." He squeezed my dad's shoulder and smiled again. "What were you pitching?" he asked.

"Betty doesn't like me to say..."

"Might as well say it and get it over with," interjected Mom. "Somebody's going to say it sooner or later, so let's just get on with it..."

"It was... uh... the... uh... *freak show*, is what we called it." I'd never seen my dad look embarrassed before. He always seemed in control of whatever situation he was in. He glanced at my mom.

"There must be a better way of describing those poor people," she said.

"See?" nodded Dad.

"So, you mean like the rubber man and the bearded lady... and...?" suggested the Reverend, using his hands descriptively.

"Yeah. Usually, I'd bring out the sword swallower to stop the crowd and then pitch them on the rest of the show to get them inside."

"Did they always go in?" I asked.

"Eventually. Sometimes we had to use a little persuasion."

"Like what?"

"Well, sometimes we'd have to bring out one of the other acts, just for a second, to tantalize them; and if that didn't work, there was always half-price for the first five people at the ticket booth."

"Did that work?"

"Pretty much all the time it did, yeah."

"Twelve-thirty," said the Reverend, looking at his watch. "We sold anything at all?"

Mrs. Smith, working the cash box, chuckled. "Only to ourselves."

Things were busy at the other end of the midway, but dead as a graveyard where we were. We were jolted out of our disappointment by the roar of a big truck pulling up on the prairie side of our tent. It was a tractor unit without the trailer, and the flowing script on the door read: *Many Miracles Ministries.*

The driver was unshaven, and in need of a haircut. He looked at our menu for a moment. "We've got a good deal," pitched Mrs. Janz. "Fifteen cents gets you a burger or a dog, and a drink. You could add ice cream for dessert. Just a nickel."

The driver replied, "I think I'll just have a burger, lots of onions, and a drink."

"Just passing through?" queried Dad.

"Nope. We're settin' up just on the other side of town. We'll be ready to save some souls as soon as the fair here shuts down.

That'd be Wednesday, right?"

Dad nodded. "You follow the rodeo circuit?"

"You bet. We've got a salvation show tonight at eight as well, and there'll be lots of folks there who don't want to hang around the fairgrounds."

"You're not the preacher, right?" asked my dad carefully.

"No, no," laughed the man, "I'm just the driver and the gofer. The Reverend John-Luke Matthews is back at the site making sure the tent gets put up properly this time. We nearly sent the whole congregation to their reward last week. Ha Ha Ha." He headed down the midway.

"How come he said he was a gopher, Dad?"

Dad laughed. "Not a gopher, a *go... fer*. It means he goes fer this and he goes fer that. A *go... fer*, get it?"

"So they can just set up a tent and hold a church service?" I asked.

"They're like the carnival, Lester," said Dad. "It's all bally. Not like our church where we have a regular minister and some-place to go if we've got trouble."

"Now, now," said Mom, "I'm sure they are a comfort to some folks."

"Whatever you say, dear," said Dad, in a resigned sort of way.

We were all quiet for a while after that. Dad stood at the front and drummed his fingers on the white oilcloth that covered the plywood counter.

"Onions are going to start burning," said Mom from the grill. "We'll have to throw them out."

Reverend Schmidtke had been in the back. He came out to suggest we take most of the hamburger patties and the wieners back downtown to the frozen food locker, before they spoiled.

"Can I go?" I asked. I loved to go to the frozen food lock-ers. It wasn't like the little freezer at the top of your fridge. You could walk right into these lockers and there were little wooden shelves going up the walls and everything was all covered in frost. Everywhere you looked, there were piles of little brown paper packages; meat that had been cut up and frozen. You could rent a locker after you had a pig butchered or something and keep all the meat there.

"You can go as long as you don't go empty-handed," allowed Dad. "Make sure you help carry as much as you can."

"I don't know what we do about tomorrow," said the Reverend.

"Think there's much point in us even opening for business?" asked my dad.

"Well…" The Reverend took a long, deep breath. "There are some expenses. We had to pay to get in on the location lottery. The Jensens donated the corn, but it looks like some of the meat will spoil, and we had to buy that. Church finances being what they are this year, we really can't afford to lose money on this."

Dad and the other men stared at the ground, and absently smoothed the grass and weeds around their feet with their boots.

"Doesn't look like anyone's going to come down this far to buy anything," somebody said timidly.

"It's too bad," came a voice from farther around the circle. "Our food is as good as anyone else's."

"Would they let us take a bunch of food in, say, a box, and carry it around the grandstand?" came another idea. "You know, how they sell peanuts and hot dogs at the ball games in the city?"

"No, someone asked that at the meeting," answered the Reverend. "The people with the tents next to the midway objected."

There were a few other suggestions, but none that amounted to anything.

"Hal," said the Reverend, thoughtfully, "you've spent a little time on the midway. Any ideas?"

"Not really. We always had control of the food concessions. We knew where to put them. And this…" He looked around.

"This is a bad spot, right?" said the Reverend, completing Dad's thought.

Dad shrugged his shoulders. "Couldn't be much worse." He smiled a sick smile.

"You know what we really need, Hal," winked the Reverend, "is a bally stand. We ought to have you out there pitching the folks on coming here to buy food. Maybe you could say these weren't regular burgers. Maybe they're... oh... uh... from special cattle... raised... in... oh... in... some... exotic place. Ha ha ha ha." My dad was grinning now.

"Lying outside of a church tent? That doesn't sound right to me," glowered Mrs. Johnson, as she wiped off the un-used counter for about the fifteenth time.

Everyone looked at the Reverend. "The Lord works in mysterious ways," he said. "How about if we called them *mystery burgers*?" He was putting on a scary voice now, rolling his R's and holding his hands up like Dracula. Everyone laughed. Except Mrs. Johnson.

"The Good Book tells us the Lord drew huge crowds with his miracles..."

"Right," said Mrs. Johnson, "but he wasn't serving hot dogs and burgers."

"No, but at one point he did serve bread and fish," replied the Reverend.

"How about fish burgers," I joked, but nobody laughed. And, I got a "behave" look from mother.

"Anyway," said the Reverend, "it was just a thought. It never hurts to just toss ideas around. We're using the brains the good Lord gave us to look for a solution to our problems."

"Sounds like a lot of foolishness to me," snapped Mrs. Johnson.

"Anyway," concluded the Reverend, "we'll see if we do any better at suppertime, and then meet here at about sevenish, to see if we can come up with a plan for tomorrow. Right now, I've got some hospital visits to make. Bless you all," he said cheerily, heading for his car.

"So, Dad," I said, "we might be losing money with our food, but there's a guy I watched over on the other side who looks like he's losing a lot of money, and he's with the carnival."

"What were you watching?" he asked.

"Well, he's got a little stage like you were talking about, and he invites people to come up there right in front of everybody. He charges them two-bits and says he can tell just by looking at them what kind of work they do. And if he's wrong – and he is most of the time – they get to pick any prize they want from the big shelves behind him."

"So," said Dad, "I know this one, but tell me exactly what you saw."

"OK. A lady pays a quarter and comes up and he looks at her hands, and then talks about her clothes and how her hair is done and some other stuff I didn't understand. Then he thinks really hard for a minute and says he believes she is a nurse. She's not. She says she is a school teacher and he invites her to pick a prize. Then a guy comes up and the fellow says he looks like a truck driver but he is really a barber, so he gets a prize too. He did get a couple of others right, though."

"Yeah, people really go for that one, because they want to win a prize," said Dad, nodding. "Here's what I want you to think about. People give him twenty-five cents in hope of winning what they think is a free prize. But he buys those prizes by the bucketload for about a nickel each, and sells them to you for a quarter, if you just stop to think about it."

He continued, "If there was a store downtown with all of those supposed prizes for two-bits each, would you rush in to buy one?"

I shook my head.

"But if you had a chance to *win* one… people forget they paid money to get something they think is for free. And everyone wants to think they got something for free."

"Ooooh, I get it. I guess it was just lucky that he got a couple of their jobs right."

"More likely," said Dad, "the ones he got right were fellow carnies up there helping him to draw in the crowd."

CHAPTER FOUR

T HE FAIRGROUND WAS BUSTLING DURING the supper hour. The bull riding had just ended and the grandstand poured out into the midway. The chariot races wouldn't begin for another hour and a half. There was a different crew staffing our tent during the supper hour, but as Cally and Dilly and I wandered past, we could see nothing was happening.

Old Mr. Janz was at the front counter. He said the only people who bought anything were those who'd parked their cars on our side of the midway. When they realized ours was the last tent they bought a burger, but we'd only sold about a dozen. The ice around the ice cream had all melted and the ice cream was being loaded into the back of Tindale's pick-up for a quick trip back to the frozen food locker. Cally and I watched as a couple of men hauled the big galvanized tub of ice-water out behind the tent and dumped it.

The meeting that night had an air of hopelessness. "I've asked if we can look for another location, but they said no," explained the Reverend, "so, we've got to make it or break it here."

"If we shut it down, how much will we lose?" someone asked.

"A couple of hundred dollars," answered the Reverend.

"Can we afford that kind of a loss?" asked Mr. Thompson.

"Unfortunately, no."

"What are we going to do?" asked Mr. Janz.

"At this point, I'm not exactly sure," said the Reverend. "I'm going to have to pray about it and sleep on it."

"You know," said Dad, "I took a walk down the midway this afternoon. I just wanted to see what people were spending their money on these days."

"And?" said Mom.

"The headless woman..."

© Eric Kitiyama/Dreamstime.com

"What? Don't tell me there's a headless woman..." started Mrs. Johnson.

"Have you walked down the midway, Penny?" he asked her.

"Well, no, I don't like crowds much, and everyone is hollering at you to come here and come there... and..."

Dad continued, "The biggest crowd is around the... uh... pardon the expression... freak show. They've got a man with alligator skin, another man with gorilla hair all over his body, and a woman with *no* head."

"That's impossible!" Mrs. Johnson was indignant. "It's got to be some kind of a fake!"

"That's very good, Penny," my dad said with just a touch of sarcasm, "but the people want a show; they want something they can look at and decide for themselves if it's real, or if it's some kind of trick. The headless woman is actually an illusion. The point is, they'll pay to try to figure it out. That's why they come to the carnival with money in their pockets."

"And your point is?" said Mrs. Johnson, returning the sarcasm.

"By the time people get to this end of the midway, they've seen all the shows, and they've already had a hamburger. They're not hungry for food; their tummies are full. My bet is, they're ready for another cheap thrill."

"So, what exactly are you saying?" asked Mr. Janz.

"I can see exactly what he's getting at," interjected the Reverend, "and I like it. I like it a lot, Hal."

"Well, please explain it to the rest of us, Reverend Schmidtke," pleaded Mrs. Johnson.

"What Hal is saying," explained the Reverend carefully, "is that we need a *headless woman.*"

"Are you out of your mind, Reverend?" Mrs. Janz stood up. She was angry. "What kind of nonsense is this?"

"Calm down, everyone, please," coaxed the Reverend. "Hal's talking figuratively here, not literally."

"Some of us don't understand what them words mean, Reverend," came a man's voice from the back.

"It means," explained the Reverend, "that we don't need a *real* headless woman. What we need is a gimmick, a trick of some kind to get people to notice our booth. That's it, isn't it, Hal?"

Dad nodded. "You *have* been around the block, haven't you?"

"What have you got in mind, Hal?" he asked.

"I dunno."

"Can you come up with something?"

"I don't know... this is a pretty tall order on short notice."

"I'm leaving it in your hands, Hal. Will you take the assignment? On behalf of the congregation, will you try to come up with something by morning?"

"I guess I could try, but I can't promise anything. It's been a long time since I... well... you know..."

"Listen, Hal," said the Reverend, "if you can't come up with something, nobody's going to hold it against you. But I've got a feeling an old carnie like you isn't going to let this opportunity for one last kick at the cat go by..."

Mrs. Johnson gasped. "That was again speaking figuratively, Mrs. Johnson," explained the Reverend.

"This gimmick you want," said Dad, "it has to be done properly. It has to look like something, even if it isn't. Whatever we come up with, we're going to need a bally stand to show it off. You can't fake people out at eye level, you understand; they have to be looking up at you. You need a little height and a little

© Loon Creative/Dreamstime.com

distance. It's all part of the game, the illusion."

"George, your boys are carpenters, aren't they?" said the Reverend to Mr. Janz.

"That's right."

"Do you suppose they've got some old lumber laying around they could knock together to make a little stage out front?"

"They've got scraps of lumber all over my back yard," he laughed. "I'll get them over here tonight to see what we can do."

"Anything else, Hal?"

"Just some kind of an idea, that's all we need now. Just an idea. Anybody?" He looked around but the faces were blank. He looked at the Reverend and made a helpless gesture with his hands.

"I'll pray for you, Hal," said the Reverend. "This meeting is adjourned."

It was a quiet ride home. Dad was deep in thought. He nearly drove through a stop sign till Mom hollered at him, and they argued about how long it took to slow down a car once the brakes were applied. Mom was still talking about how we could all have been killed when we got to our house. We had just pulled into the driveway when Dad scared everyone out of their wits. "I've got it!" he said. "The most exciting thing anyone can do is look death right in the eye and walk away!"

"What are you talking about?" asked Mom.

"Lester, what are the three musketeers up to tonight?"

That surprised me. Other people called us that, but my parents never had. "Well, not much, I guess."

"Do you think your two friends are brave enough to go down to the river caves? It'll be dark soon."

"What do you mean, brave enough? We've been down there before in the dark. It's no big deal. What do you want us to do?"

"Bring me back a headless woman. Ask your friends to come over and I'll explain to all of you at once."

CHAPTER FIVE

THAT WAS HOW WE HAPPENED to be out that night, on a quest for what my dad would always call "the headless woman". The task seemed easy enough, although it did include one element we had never tried before. We were sure we could figure it out, based on a plan Dad had suggested to us. Other than that, it was just a camping trip we'd already done a few times before. We had our bedrolls tied to our bike baskets, and our BB guns slung over our backs. We brought them along in the hope that we could get some more target practice in before we faced the balloon prize wall at the carnival, maybe tomorrow.

It was now half past eight. There was about an hour of sunlight left, and it took just under an hour to get down to the river campgrounds on our bikes. We'd done that run in itself, every Sunday afternoon, for months. We'd bike along with one eye on the road and the other in the ditch, watching for beer bottles. People used to drive along drinking on Saturday night, and then wing the empties out the window. The ditch had lots of weeds to cushion them, and the bottles never broke. By the time we'd been down to River Park and then come back on the other side of the road we always had a couple of dozen beer bottles.

Monday, after school, we'd haul them to the back door of the liquor vendor's and collect twenty-five cents a dozen. Then we'd reward ourselves with a cherry-custard ice cream cone.

The road was paved most of the way and we expected an easy ride. A mile out of town, we saw it: the biggest tent we had ever seen. It had what appeared to be two center poles. It looked like a huge circus tent. "I didn't know there was a circus coming to town," puffed Cally, pedaling along.

© A.G.M./Dreamstime.com

"I wonder if they have elephants or those fancy ponies," said Dilly. "Maybe we could get a job doing something to help pay for... that... broken..." Cally had shot him a glance and he didn't bother finishing the sentence.

"It's not a circus," I said, catching up with them, "it's some kind of a traveling preacher show. Their driver was at the midway handing out little posters." As we got closer, we could hear the faint sound of an organ over the roar of the big generator behind the tent. Then we could hear preaching. Wild preaching. Not like Reverend Schmidtke. He never screamed like that.

"I want to see," coaxed Dilly. "Let's take a look."

"Maybe," I said, "but we can't lose our sunlight. We'll just take a minute."

There were some cars in the field by the tent, and when we peeked inside, there was just a small group of people scattered among the fold-up chairs and wooden benches.

"Now, I've warned you about the demon rum and the temptations of the flesh!" the man at the front exhorted. "What I want you to do, now, is come down close to the front. Clo-o-o-ose to the front. Everybody please get up and move down close to the front, so the people who come in later don't have to squeeze by you. That's it, sir, you too; please, that's it, everybody move up close to the front. Make room for the next group at the back. That's it. Now, I want to open to the Book of..."

"Hi, boys," he smiled warmly. "Come on in." We didn't move. "Your folks here with you?" he asked, looking past us into the parking lot.

"Let's split," said Cally.

THE RIDING WAS easier now. It was pretty much a slight downhill grade all the way to the river. We rode in silence. As we rounded a curve, I sang out, "We're half way there!"

"Hold up, you guys," shouted Dilly. We looked back and he was stopped.

"What's wrong?" Cally yelled back.

"Flat tire!" called out Dilly, pointing at his front tire.

We rode back. "This is a problem," said Cally. " We haven't got any time to waste. The sun will be going down, soon."

We all carried patches and pumps, but it took a good half hour to repair a tire. We thought of ditching Dilly's bike and riding double, but Dilly's was the only one with balloon tires. Mine and Cally's were too thin, especially when we'd soon be on gravel. No one mentioned leaving Dilly there as the sun started to set and carrying on with just the two of us.

"I think we should use the daylight to fix the tire," I said.

"Then what?" said Cally. "We can't ride in the dark." Our bikes had head lamps powered by a little generator that rubbed against the front tire, but they only worked when you were going fast. As soon as you slowed down, you were biking blind.

"There is another way down to the river," I said. "The old dirt road we used to take before they put this one through."

"My dad says that road was blocked last year," said Dilly. "My aunt wanted him to take it last summer to go picking berries, and he said there were roadblocks, and a sign saying it wasn't safe."

"Not safe for cars, probably," I said. "If we fix the bike and then leave all of them in the trees over there, we can hike down to the river and get what we came for. In the morning, we'll hike back up and collect our bikes and get home. What do you say?"

Dilly threw his bike on its side, and got out his tools. It was lucky there was a full moon, because the sun went down a few minutes before we were finished.

"Full moon," said Cally. "Maybe we can keep riding." As if in heavenly contradiction, clouds scudded over and blotted out the moonlight.

"Flashlights," said Cally, whipping off his backpack. "We've all got flashlights, right?"

"We were supposed to be there before dark, and my batteries are dead. I didn't have time to get any more," replied Dilly.

"I have one, but it's the same batteries we had on the last trip," I said. I flicked the switch. Nothing. The clouds covering the moon were thinning out a bit. "Come on," I said, "I remember the way. If we cut right through these trees and go over that small rise, we'll come to the old road. We'll have enough moonlight to make it. Come on."

I was sure I remembered the way, but breathed a secret sigh of relief when we came out of the trees and onto the dirt road.

The old sign was still there: RIVER PARK - TWO MILES. We trudged along in the dark, the moon and the clouds teasing us with moments of illumination and long periods of darkness.

We hadn't gone very far when Cally noticed the car in the trees. Someone in it was lighting a cigarette. "See that?" he said. "Somebody parked in the trees."

"Why would somebody drive their car in there?" asked Dilly.

We stood still for a moment. Cally suggested we go over for a closer look.

"What if he chases us?" asked Dilly.

"We shoot him," said Cally.

"With BB guns?" I asked.

"Would you want to stand up against three of them?" he replied.

"You could have a point," I said.

"Unless the guy has a real gun in the car," countered Cally.

We walked softly along the road, hoping to just get by without being noticed. The window rolled down, and we could hear the radio as a cigarette butt was flicked in our general direction. We stood stock-still, not wanting to be seen. Although no one said it, we were afraid to even know who could be parked out there in the trees in the dark. "Maybe it's some kind of bogeyman just waiting for someone to come along and pounce on," suggested Dilly.

"He'd wait for a long time on this road," said Cally. "It's not supposed to be in use, remember?"

Then we could hear a girl's voice. She got louder and it was obvious they were arguing about something. "That's my sister," said a surprised Cally. "That's Susan!"

"You sure?" I asked.

"Of course I'm sure. She told Mom she was sleeping over with a friend tonight."

Said Dilly sarcastically, "Looks like maybe she was telling the truth."

"Cool it, you guys, or they'll hear us," I warned.

Just about then Dilly slipped and fell into a ditch. "You all right?" I asked.

"Yes, but watch your step; it drops off real fast."

We followed him down into the ditch. He was sitting on a thick bed of leaves and we sat down beside him. "What do you want to do, Cally?" I asked.

"*Do*? Why would he want to do anything?" said Dilly. "Let's just get out of here!"

"No way," said Cally. "My sister shouldn't be in that car. Not after what happened with Julie."

"Who's Julie?" I asked.

"My oldest sister. She's a couple of years older than Susan."

"I guess I haven't seen her around," I said.

"I guess *not*," said Cally, in his often smart-mouth way. "She was in grade eleven when they sent her away to live with my aunt. She used to park in cars with guys, too. Susan promised Mom she'd never do that."

We were quiet for a moment. "You have to keep promises," said Cally, with an air of finality.

"John Wayne says a man's word is his bond," said Dilly. "That's what the Duke says."

"John Wayne? John Wayne? You believe a cowboy in the movies? My dad says he's not even a real cowboy. You go to too many matinees," said Cally. Then he suddenly stood up and shouted, "Keep your promise, Susan! Keep your promise!" He was almost crying, he was so upset.

"Get down, Cally," I said. "You don't want to take on her boyfriend if he comes after you."

Dilly was peeking over the edge of the ditch. "He didn't hear anything. They've got the radio on loud. Listen - you can hear it."

"I don't care," said Cally. "I'll fight him! I'll fight him! I don't care how big he is! Leave my sister alone!" he shouted. Cally was rooting around in the dirt with his hands. He found an egg-sized rock and stood up. "Leave my sister alone!" He threw the rock and ducked back down.

Whonk! The rock hit the car. We heard the door creak open. "Who's out there?" came an angry voice through the trees.

"You've done it now," said Dilly. "He's probably going to kill us."

We could hear the boyfriend moving around in the brush. "Who's out there?" he demanded.

Cally picked up another rock. "Oh, no," said Dilly, "you're not serious..."

"I'm not afraid of anybody!" He measured out the words and then stood up. "We're coming to kill you, jerk face!" he shouted, lobbing the rock high above his head.

Whonk! The second rock hit the car. "I'm scared, Jerry!" wailed Susan through the night. "Let's get out of here!"

We lay huddled in the ditch as the car door slammed and the motor roared to life. He gunned it in reverse into the road, and then spun the car around; its headlights now pointing directly over our heads.

We didn't even breathe. He sat there for a moment, gunning his engine in anger. Then he turned the car to the left and sat there for a moment, then slowly he turned it right again, arcing his high beams directly over us.

"You better hope I never catch you!" he shouted furiously out of his open window into the darkness. Then he gunned his engine and sprayed rocks and dirt all over us as he tore off down the road, heading back towards town.

We climbed up out of the dirt. "Did you hear the clunk when those rocks landed?" asked Cally. "Wait'll he tries to explain that to his old man."

"Yeah," said Dilly, "he'll probably have to go pick beans for the summer to pay off the damage."

"What happens if we ever find out who broke the Martin's window?" asked Cally.

"I don't know."

"We kill them," said Cally, as casual as if he had just said he was going in for supper.

"You wouldn't actually kill a *person*, would you?" asked Dilly.

"You couldn't even kill that sparrow!" replied Cally. "You got sick. We had to finish it off for you."

"I could have finished it off if I had wanted to..."

"You were puking your guts out, man..."

"It was not because of that."

"Oh, really. What was it then?"

"I think I ate something bad..."

Cally mocked him in falsetto. "I think I ate something bad, I think I ate something bad and it made me sick... so-o-o-o-o sick..."

Dilly jumped in with, "Let's go get the headless lady."

"Well, we know where they should be," I said. "It should be easy to bring one back."

"Your old man is pretty cool," said Cally, over his shoulder. Then he walked backwards for a few steps as he spoke. "This is going to be neat."

"You think this plan is going to work?" I asked.

"Oh ya. I love it."

WE PICKED OUR way along the dark dirt road for a few more minutes, and then we heard a long howling sound that made the hair on the backs of our necks stand on end. "Coyotes," whispered Cally. "Those are coyotes."

"Good thing we've got our guns," whispered Dilly.

"Why are you whispering?" asked Cally.

"Because you were, Doofus!" came the reply.

"I was not!"

"You were so! Wasn't he whispering, Fester?"

"You're scared, Dilly," taunted Cally.

"I am not!"

"Look out behind you, Dilly! A coyote - he's charging!"

"Ahhhhhhh!" Dilly screamed. He was running and trying to

look behind him at the same time. "Where is it? Where is it?" he screamed. "Get it away from me! Don't let it bite me!"

"Ha ha ha ha ha," laughed Cally. "Told you, you were scared!"

Dilly stopped running. "I knew there was no coyote." Dilly's voice was quavering. "I was just playing along. Having some fun."

"Ya, right," said Cally. "You *sounded* like you were having some fun, all right."

"Anyway," said Dilly, "if those coyotes do come close, we've got our guns. I think I'm going to load mine right now," he added, pulling it off his shoulder.

"You think a BB gun is going to bother a coyote?" scoffed Cally.

"I'll bet you could kill one if you got him right in the eye. It would go right into his brain and kill him. I read that's how they kill some animals in Africa."

"For you to get a shot at his eye, he'd pretty much have to have his teeth around your face, Dilly," said Cally, disgustedly.

"Maybe if they just see we have guns, they'll back off," hoped Dilly.

"You think coyotes know what guns look like?" I asked as we trudged along in the semi-moonlight.

"They might, they're scared of guns," said Dilly.

"Scared of the sound, maybe," I said. "I mean, say coyotes *did* know what guns looked like, would they know the difference between a 30/30 and a BB gun? Do they know that's where the sound comes from?"

"How would a coyote know what a gun looks like? The only ones who might know are obviously dead," said Cally.

"Coyotes can't read," I said. "So, even if they did know what a gun looked like, they couldn't tell what kind it was."

"So how would a coyote know what a gun looked like in the first place?" said Cally. "That's what I want to know."

"They'd have to see one," suggested Dilly. "Maybe in a catalogue."

Cally was at his sarcastic best now. "Like coyotes get the Spring and Summer Catalogue from Sears, Dilly."

"Maybe a camper left one behind," offered Dilly.

"Sure, and a coyote came along and sat down and thumbed through it, probably ordered some winter underwear, and then said, 'Oh, look. Here is the gun section. I'll have to show this to every coyote I know'. Is that what you think happens, Dilly?"

"No, that would be stupid. Know why?"

"Of course, because it never happened."

"No, that's not why."

"Why, then?" Cally sounded exasperated.

"Because you can't get winter underwear from the Summer Catalogue!"

"That's it!" said Cally. "You're dead!" He lunged at Dilly, and Dilly took off running. Cally was hot on his heels. I loped along, just trying to keep them in sight.

It had often seemed to me that the verbal abuse Cally heaped on his friends was his way of showing some kind of strength. We knew he didn't mean anything by it, and it wasn't as though anyone ever held a grudge because of anything that was said. Cally's dad had been a boxer before he got hurt in the ring and went into the hardware business. At least, that's what everyone said. All he ever kept telling Cally was, "Never back down. Never back down from a fight. Stand your ground like a man. Never let anyone see you cry." Stuff like that.

Even when Cally was wrong, he would never apologize. When we asked him why, he said it was a sign of weakness. We asked if his dad had also told him that, but he had said, "No, he learned that in a movie from John Wayne."

* ** * ** * **

"HERE IT IS!" I heard Cally shout in the moonlight. "Come on, Fester!"

After a moment I could see the faint outline of a barricade across the road. The sign said DANGER. We stood there for a minute, waiting for enough moonlight to see what was on the other side, when Dilly said, "Look over there. Through the trees. Somebody's house. You can see their lights."

He was right. From what we could make out, it was an old-looking cabin. The ground around it was overgrown with weeds and it looked like no one had lived in it for years. "Sounds like a car coming," said Cally. We looked behind us and could see headlights strobing through the trees. Once it rounded the curve he'd be coming right at us. We ran into the trees and watched. The car's headlights had picked up the barricades, but it didn't seem to be slowing down. "Is he going to crash right through?" asked Cally. "Maybe the guy's drunk or something."

When the car reached the barricades, it braked suddenly and turned right, seeming to disappear into the trees. "There must be a road going off to the right," said Dilly.

"You guys didn't notice one?" I asked. Both said no.

"Someone must live up there now," I said.

We watched through the trees as the car came to a halt, and the lights went out. We heard the car door open, and then close again. Close to where it had parked, another set of headlights came on, and a car started back down in our direction. Once again we melted into the trees. As it came out onto the road its headlights lit up what were really ruts going into the old farm house. The headlights also lit up the other side of the barricade and showed us the road looked pretty rough.

"Another car," said Cally. It was another one coming in, but as it got closer we could see it was actually a pick-up. It slowed down long before it got to the barricades, and used a spotlight to search the trees for the opening. When they found it, the driver bounced over the ruts, and two guys in the back hollered at him to watch out.

"Cowboys," said Cally. "And they sound like they're drunk."

"How can you tell if they're drunk?" asked Dilly, a strong tone of disbelief in his voice.

"Listen to them," replied Cally. "You can hear them from here."

We could. They were at the cabin. We saw the truck lights go out, but we could hear them hollering about something, and laughing like the devil. "What do you suppose is going on up there?" Cally wondered.

"Want to see if we can get close enough to find out?" I asked.

"Maybe Dilly's too scared," said Cally.

"And maybe Dilly's *not!*" he retorted.

"You think we've got time?" asked Cally.

"We've got all night," I replied. "It's either this or lie in the tent listening to the coyotes thumb through the catalogue."

Dilly struck out through the trees first.

CHAPTER SIX

I FOUND OUT LATER THAT Dad was just putting the finishing touches on his pitch for the "headless woman", and Mom was knitting, when they heard the screaming outside in the darkness. Dad opened the front door and looked out. In the glow of the streetlight, he could see a young man running along, holding his right shoulder with his left hand. "You all right?" shouted Dad.

"Something bit me," answered the young man, a note of panic in his voice.

"You mean a dog bit you?"

"No, I think it was a snake. I didn't really see it, though."

"Did he say a snake?" asked Mom.

"That's what it sounded like, but there are no snakes in town. They're down in the coulees by the river."

"Where the *boys* are going? I told you to drive them down there."

"Relax, they're all right," he said, glancing at his watch. "By now they're in the tent telling ghost stories. They need some time away from us and this will be fun for them."

"When are you going to tell me what you sent them down there for?"

"You'll see in the morning, if they can do it, and I think they can. I just don't want anybody to know but me, in case it doesn't work out."

The young man was coming up the front walk now. "I feel really sick. Can anybody help me?"

Dad stepped out on the front step, and caught the young man's arm, steadying him. "Where were you bitten?"

"Right here," he was starting to sob, "on my shoulder."

Dad unbuttoned the young man's shirt, noting how filthy it was. There was dirt and grease on it, as though it hadn't been washed for a month. The young man was also in need of a shave and a haircut, not to mention a bath. Dad slipped the shirt off the man's shoulder and looked at the double wound. "You've been snake bit, all right. This happened just down the street from here?"

"Yeah. Just down about three houses."

"That's...um...really odd. Come on, I'll drive you to Doc Campbell's house. Wait. Betty, do you want to call and make sure he's home?"

While she dialed, Dad said, "I've never seen a snake in town. They've got everything they need down by the river. How'd you get bit in the shoulder?"

"Ah... I was, uh, out for a walk, and ... uh... my watch fell off and I bent down to pick it up and got bit."

"Maybe you can show me where it happened, so we can go out there and see if it's still around."

"Yeah, sure. Oh, it hurts, it hurts."

Mom came to the door. "Anita says Mac's out on a call, and no one else there knows how to handle a snake bite, but they're going to look it up in a book, or something. Anita says she'll send Mac to the hospital as soon as he gets home, or he may stop there on the way just to see what's happening. She thinks you ought to get him to the hospital right now. Snake bites are serious."

"I *know* how serious snake bites are, thank you."

Dad had intended to drive him to the hospital, but his car wouldn't start. The gas gauge was on empty. He had thought he still had a quarter tank left. "No matter," he said, "it's only a few blocks. We can walk it." As they set off, Dad said, "I haven't seen you around here before."

"No, uh, I'm from out of town."

"Just in for the fair?"

"Ya."

* * *   * * *   * * *

"I DON'T THINK we should go any closer," warned Cally. We had reached the trees along the edge of an old farmyard, and for some reason it was very busy. There were about ten cars and pick-ups in the yard, and we could see men handing over money for quart sealers.

"Moonshine," I said. "They're buying moonshine. Must be a still out here, somewhere."

"That's not all that's going on," said Dilly. "Look over there."

Two men were fighting in the corner of the yard. A woman got out of one of the cars and tried to stop them, and one of the men hit her in the head with something. She went down like a sack of potatoes.

"Look what you did!" shouted one of the men.

"It was an accident," shouted the other. "I didn't mean to hit her. I didn't even know she was there!"

"Help me get her inside. The Doc's in there."

"She looks like she's dead."

"No, she's breathing. She's just unconscious."

They hauled her inside. We worked our way around the yard through the trees, until we could see inside. The room was lit by a kerosene lamp. It was them, all right. They were looking down and shaking their heads. "They must have laid her on a couch," said Dilly.

"Brilliant," replied Cally.

"Look, it's Doc Campbell coming into the room," I said. "I

wonder what he's doing out here?"

"Look what he's got in his hand," said Cally, as the doctor raised the quart sealer to his lips. Then he screwed the top back on the jar and appeared to put it down. He bent over for a moment, perhaps to examine the woman, then straightened up quickly and left the room. A moment later he came out the front door, with his flashlight and walked right past us to his car. He opened the door, reached in for his black bag, and hurried back into the house.

"Maybe he's going to operate," said Dilly. "I want to see."

"More likely he's just going to give her some smelling salts," I said.

"I don't care, I still want to see. I'm going in closer."

"Me too," said Cally.

"Let's stay behind the cars and keep down. We don't want to get caught out here," I cautioned. As we got closer, we could see the window was broken. Most of the glass was on the ground. We carefully crawled right over to the side of the house and sat with our backs to the wall. I thought we had left our gear in the trees, but Dilly still had his gun. "What did you bring that for?" I whispered.

"Shut up, you never know when you might need it. Randolph Scott says you always keep your back to the wall and your rifle ready."

"Randolph Scott?" I said. "The cowboy in the movies?"

"Yes, but he's a real cowboy."

"I doubt it," said Cally. "He's just an actor."

"No way, he's real," argued Dilly. "Anyway, I've got my gun and you guys haven't, so if anything happens it'll be your funeral."

"I guess we'll just have to depend on a professional gun-fighter like you to protect us," I teased.

"Maybe I will, and maybe I won't," whispered Dilly defiantly. "I'm going to see what's happening."

Dilly moved over to the side of the window and very slowly stood up, flat against the wall. Cally and I stood up on the other side, barely daring to breathe as we peeked through the window. The doctor looked like he was pushing the woman's eyelids open or something. We couldn't really tell. Suddenly, she came to and thrashed her arms around, knocking the doctor's open bag off the arm of the couch and spilling part of its contents on the floor beside her.

"What are you doing to me?" she screamed. "Get away from me, you animals!"

Dilly put his face full in the broken window to see what was going to happen next. The woman picked something shiny off the floor. She leaned back to aim it at the doctor who now had his back to us. The moonlight glinted off what looked like a little silver dart as she angrily threw it at it him. He stepped aside, and Dilly pulled his face quickly away from the window. He stood against the wall for just a second, and then slowly slid down, his legs buckling under him heading for the broken glass. I jumped over and caught him on the way down and pushed him to where there was no glass. Cally grabbed his BB gun before it clattered to the ground.

He was lying there in the dirt, not making a move.

"Dilly! What's wrong?" I was trying not to be too loud.

"What happened to him?" asked Cally excitedly. It was too dark to see what had happened. Then the clouds parted and the moonlight revealed a little pair of silver scissors. They were stuck in Dilly's forehead like a pickle fork.

CHAPTER SEVEN

"I WONDER IF WE SHOULD pull them out," I said. "You'd pull a sliver out. Maybe it's the same thing."

"But you've never had a sliver that big in the middle of your forehead," said Cally. "What if his brains leak out or something?"

"I don't think that's how it works."

"Weren't you telling us what a big man you were for getting your first-aid badge in Scouts?" whispered Cally furiously. "Do something!"

"We didn't cover scissors stuck in the head. *You* do something!"

In the moonlight, I could see Dilly was still breathing; but his eyes were closed. I could also see that Cally's face was glistening just a little. "You all right?" I asked.

"I don't feel so good. I feel like I'm sweating. What if he dies, man? I mean, what if he lays right here on the ground and dies? What do we do then, huh?"

"We'd better get the doctor," I said.

Cally stood up to look in the window. "I can't see anything

– there's no light in the room. They must have taken the lamp with them. That means we're going to have to go in the house and find him... Oh Oh."

"What?"

"There's a pick-up coming in. It's heading over this way. There are cars parked around the back too, so we'd better move Dilly so he doesn't get run over." I held Dilly under the shoulders and Cally was between his legs, holding him under the knees. Cally had slung Dilly's gun over his back and we sort of half carried, half dragged him between a couple of parked cars. "This is the doctor's car," observed Cally. "Let's just lay him close beside it, and then you can go and ask the doctor to come out to his car."

"*I* should go?"

"One of us should stay with Dilly, and I really don't feel so good."

The pick-up had stopped for a moment, right in front of us. The driver looked around, but he didn't see us. We were on the ground between the doctor's car and someone else's, well below his eye level. The pick-up slowly moved forward and drove up close against the trees, where it was quite dark. We watched the driver get out and take something from the back of the truck. Then he started walking towards the front of the house. If we had stayed where we were, we would have been caught for sure. The clouds parted a bit, and we could see he was carrying some type of can. It had a handle on it and a spout. He stopped near the front of the house and unscrewed a cap from the spout; then he began pouring something along the bottom of the house, and sloshed some of it up on the porch. He was muttering to himself. We couldn't make out much of it, but it sounded like, "Cleanse by fire, cleanse by fire..."

"What's that mean?" whispered Cally.

"I don't know. The guy must be crazy."

Then he got louder. "The purveyors of the demon drink will burn!"

"You know who that is?" said Cally.

"Who?"

"It's that preacher. The one from the tent we stopped at."

"You think so? I never got a good look at him."

"I did. That's him."

"So what's he doing?"

"That can is the same kind my Grandpa keeps his kerosene in, for his lamps." The man had stopped pouring now, and threw the can on the ground. "Fire and brimstone," he said excitedly, patting his vest pocket. Then he put his hands in his jacket pockets. Then he checked his pants pockets. "What's he looking for?" wondered Cally.

"What if it's a match?" I said.

"A match?"

"Yeah. What if that *is* kerosene? I mean, what else would he be pouring around out there?"

"Holy cow! I'll bet you're right."

The preacher was muttering something to himself as he headed back to his truck. He was rummaging around in the cab when a cowboy came out of the front door. He had a quart sealer in his hand and a cigarette in his mouth. We could barely see him there in the dark.

"You *going*?" asked Cally.

"In a minute. I don't want anyone to know we're here."

"They'll know we're here when you knock on the door, stupid. Are you afraid to go?"

"Just wait a minute, O.K.?"

"You're scared, aren't you?"

"I'll go in just a second, O.K.?"

"No, you're scared. I'll go. I'm not scared of anything."

We crouched there for a moment. We couldn't see the cowboy any more, but we did see the bright red glow in the dark as he took a long last drag on his cigarette. Then he plucked it from his mouth and flicked the butt away from him. We saw the glowing red ember fall to the ground, and then, *WHOOMPF!*

The grass instantly caught fire and a little river of flame

raced towards the house and ran up inside the little porch. Then it became a bright fire. The cowboy shouted something we couldn't make out and ran along the side of the house and disappeared in the dark. The preacher jumped up and down shouting, "Fire from heaven! The Lord's vengeance. Blessed be the na-a-a-a-me of the Lo-o-o-ord!"

Now people were hopping out the side window. They stopped long enough to have a quick look at the blaze. "Nothing we can do," someone shouted, and people raced for their cars and drove quickly out of the yard. The car beside us started up, so Cally and I left Dilly on the ground and ran to the other side of the doctor's car, not wanting to be seen. Then we realized the doctor was already at his car. We ran around the back of it, and got back to the driver's side in time to see him open the car door. The bottom of the door hit the handle of the scissors, and they popped out of Dilly's forehead and onto the ground. The doctor hadn't noticed Dilly, and when he went to get into the car, he stepped right on Dilly's arm.

"Ahhhhh!" groaned Dilly.

"What the...?" The doctor was shocked. Then he saw us. "What are you boys doing out here at this time of the night? You have no business out here."

"We're... sort of... camping," I said. "And Dilly's been hurt. I was just coming in to get you."

The doctor lifted Dilly into the front seat. He turned on the dome light, but the fire was brighter. "How did this happen?" he asked, looking back and forth at the wound and then us and then the fire.

"The scissors that woman tossed at you," said Cally. "They stuck right in his forehead."

The doctor's eyes got wide. "You boys must have been right at the window. Look," the doctor had a worried expression on his face now, "there's no need to mention who you saw out here

44

tonight. I'll take care of... uh... this is the Brock boy, isn't it?" We nodded. "Yes, I know his mom," he said. Then, "Do you boys know anything about this fire?"

"The preacher from that big tent at the edge of town poured kerosene or something along the building," said Cally. "That's him over there just getting into his truck." The doctor's car and the pick-up were the only ones left in the yard now, and the pick-up was turning around, headed our way.

"You saw him pour the kerosene?"

"Yes, we did. Right on the house," I said.

"It must have been pretty dark then. How can you be sure it was him?"

"It sounded like him," said Cally.

"But you didn't actually see his face?"

"We sorta saw his face, a bit," said Cally. "Should we tell the sheriff?"

"If you only saw him before the fire it was probably too dark. It'll never stand up in court," said the doctor. "I testified in a case just the other day that happened in the dark, and the guy got off. Identification was not positive. That's what the judge said."

"So what do we do?" I asked.

"When he goes by, get his license number," advised the doctor.

As the truck approached, we stared hard at the front license plate but could not make out the number in the dark. "Take a good look at the truck," said the doctor. "Look for some identifying mark on it."

"It's too dark," I said. "We can't even tell what make it is, or even what color for sure. And all the smoke isn't helping!"

"You want an identifying mark," said Cally resolutely, "I'll give you an identifying mark." As the rear of the truck went by, he levered Dilly's gun and put it to his shoulder. *Pap!* We heard the BB hit: *THWAK!*

"That oughta do it," said Cally.

"Nice thought, son," said the doctor, "but you can hardly go

45

looking for a truck with a tiny dent in it no bigger than a rock chip in the paint."

"Just wait," said Cally. "I aimed for his tail-light."

As the truck slowed down to make the turn, we could see the dim red tail-lights. Then he hit the brakes to turn left onto the ruts, and the tail-lights became bright. In the middle of the driver's side tail-light was a bright little white crack.

"Very good…very good…ha ha ha ha… I would never have thought of doing that," chuckled the doctor. You boys want a ride back to town?"

"No, we've got our bikes down the road," I said. "We're going to stay for a while."

The fire was starting to die down. "That's odd," said the doctor. "It looks like just the front of the house is going to burn. It's going out for some reason." We watched as the flames turned to thick smoke. "Maybe I should at least take the boy, here, home," the doctor offered.

"No," protested Dilly. "I don't want to go home."

"How's your head?" asked the doctor.

"It's hurting something awful, but I'll be all right."

"Here," said the doctor, opening his black bag. "Take a couple of these. You boys got any water?"

"Canteens are with our stuff," said Cally. "I'll go." He ran into the trees. The front end of the house was just smoldering now.

Doctor Campbell peeled back the bandage he had applied. "Well, you're not bleeding any more, and it's really just a nick, but I think you're going to have some nice purple bruising before you're done."

Dilly touched his hand to his forehead. "Ow, that hurts when I touch it. Oh, does that hurt."

"Maybe a little bone chip. You get in and let me have a close look at that as soon as you can. What do you want me to tell your mother?"

"Don't tell her anything," begged Dilly. "I'll just tell her I fell off my bike, or something…"

46

"Well, I've got to get back to town," said the doctor. Dilly slowly got out of the car. "You're sure you're going to be all right?" the doctor asked.

"Yeah. I'll be fine," Dilly assured, weakly.

We watched as the doctor drove out of the yard and bounced over the ruts and out of sight. Sitting in the trees with our gear, I said, "What should we do now?"

"I just want to lay here for a while," said Dilly. "This is going to be the first time we've been camping and didn't have a campfire."

"What do you call that?" asked Cally, pointing to the house. There were still lots of glowing embers. "Hey, we've got some wieners. Want to roast them?"

"NO!" said Dilly. "Not in the ashes of somebody's house. That wouldn't be right, would it?"

"I don't know," said Cally. "I've never thought about it."

We moved back into the trees with our bedrolls, watching the burned timbers glow and then die. The moonlight made eerie shapes of the wisps of smoke that rose from the charred timbers.

"Look at that white smoke over there," I said. "It looks like the Genie from Aladdin's lamp. Look at the shape. It looks just like the cartoon in my little sister's book."

"What if there really was a Genie," said Dilly. "What would you wish for?"

"I don't know," I said.

"Me neither," echoed Cally.

We were silent for a while, contemplating. Then I asked, "What about you, Dilly? What would you wish for?"

"Well…," he paused.

"Well, what?" said Cally. "Tell us."

"You'd think it was stupid."

"We think most of what you say is stupid," said Cally. "Why should this be any different, Dilly?"

"Well, you see, that's *it*," replied Dilly.

"What's it?" asked Cally.

"Dilly."

"Dilly? That's your name. What are you afraid of, we're going to wear it out?" laughed Cally.

"My name isn't Dilly, it's Peter."

"No, man, your name is Dilly. What are you saying? Do you want us to start calling you Peter, Peter, Pumpkin Eater, had a wife and couldn't keep 'er?"

"No, just Peter. Or maybe Pete."

"I like Dilly," said Cally. "That's always been your name. Always will."

"It's just that..."

"Just what, Dilly?" I asked.

"We're going back to school in a few weeks... and I thought that... maybe..."

"You think you're getting too big for your britches. You think you're getting too big to be called Dilly. That's it, isn't it?" scorned Cally.

"It's just that there will be other people around, you know..."

"Other people...ohhhhhh," said Cally. "I get it now. Other people. He means *girls*!"

"No. No. No," protested Dilly. "That's not it!"

"Yes, it is," said Cally. "He doesn't want the girls calling him Dilly. So, tell us, who have you got your eye on, huh?"

"Nobody. Nobody."

"You liar!" laughed Cally. He threw his bedroll at Dilly and hit him in the face. Dilly rolled over in pain. "Oh, man, I'm sorry. I'm sorry. I didn't mean it. I didn't mean to hurt you, man."

Dilly groaned.

"What can I do, man? Come on, Dilly, what can I do to make it better? I'll do anything. Anything."

"Anything?" asked Dilly.

"Yes. Honest."

"Then stop calling me Dilly. Call me Peter or even Pete, but not Dilly."

"That's going to be strange," said Cally. "You don't look like a Pete. You look like a Dilly."

"You promised."

"O.K. Pete...Pete... Pete... I don't think it fits you at all. What do you think, Fester?" asked Cally.

I had been quiet through this whole discussion. Dilly - or *Pete* - was sounding a lot like my mother and that bothered me. She was, after all, an adult; and here was Dilly - or Peter - now thinking like her. At least, he was *talking* like her.

I finally offered, "My mother doesn't think people should be called by anything other than their real names. She even got upset when I told her we had to meet in front of the Chinaman's to go pick beans."

"What's wrong with that?" asked Cally.

"Well, the way she sees it, and you have to understand *I'm* not saying this, O.K., this is just my *mother*, right? She says when we go to get our shoes fixed, we go to Mr. Pappadapa ... how do you say his name? Anyhow, you know who I mean. He's Greek."

"So?"

"So, when you go to get your shoes fixed, where do you say you're going?"

Cally shrugged. "To the shoemaker's, I guess."

"How come you don't say you're going to the Greek's? This is just what my mother would ask, O.K. ?"

"Ya. I guess..."

"So, how come? How come you don't say you're going to the Greek's?"

"I dunno."

"When you get your hair cut, where do you go?"

"To the barbershop. What kind of stupid riddles are these? You're telling us stupid riddles you got from your mother? Oh, man."

"No, see, my mom says Mr. Gionelli is Italian. But you don't say you're going to the Italian's. You say you're going to the bar- bershop, right?"

"Your old lady is stupid, Fester. You can't tell where some- body is from just by looking at them, except for the Chinaman."

"I tried that one on my mom, and she said, 'How do you know he wasn't born right here in Rascal River?'"

"I don't care what your old lady says. It's not a big deal."

"My mom says it might be a big deal to the Chinaman."

"What does she think we ought to call him? How about... Dilly? Dilly's available now. If she doesn't like us to call him the Chinaman, we'll call him Dilly, how about that?" he laughed.

"Actually, my mom says his name is George Fong. 'Fong's Fine Foods' the sign says," I replied.

"I can read," said Cally. "And I know more about him than you do."

"Like what?"

"Like when the builders come into my dad's store to get lumber and they tell him where they're putting up a new house, somebody always says, 'How far is it from the Chinaman's?'"

"Why?"

"How should I know? Maybe they're worried about how far they'll have to walk to get a quart of milk."

"All I know is…" I said, trying to put the matter to rest, "my mom says when we call him the Chinaman it's like making fun of him or not showing respect or something and we shouldn't do that."

* * *   * * *   * * *

BACK IN TOWN, George Fong's thoughts mirrored what the boys were saying in some ways. Yes, he knew many referred to him as the Chinaman, but some of the other business owners called him George or Mr. Fong. Things had improved a bit after the war. After he and some of his immigrant countrymen had served as soldiers, the Chinese were then allowed to vote.

There were two Chinese restaurants in Rascal River and they had a lot of regular customers. Most people said how much they liked the food, but there were some who were not so complimentary. Maybe they were just trying to be funny, with no thought of how it might hurt. Like the fellow who said to his friends. "You know what it sounds like when they are talking in Chinese to each other? It sounds like this…" And he held a handful of coins in the air and dropped then on the table.

Even so, George was doing all he could to become a part of the community he would one day bring his wife from China to join. He always tried to be helpful at a town event and never complained or asked for any favors.

As he would visit the restaurants to eat and visit to fight off the loneliness he often felt late in the evening, they supported him by buying various Chinese medicines he would bring in. Some of the townspeople were also showing some very cautious interest and that was helping his business grow just a little.

As he thought about all of this tonight, he was restocking the shelves and mopping the floor of the store. Some children with muddy shoes had come in with their mom and he knew the place had to look clean in the morning.

After that he would look at sales he had made that day, what his expenses were, and the tiny profit. What little bit was left over he would send to China, to help his wife.

With all of that done, he could finally relax and start reading letters from home, often exhausted, he would fall asleep while doing so.

* * *   * * *   * * *

"Hmmm. Look at Dilly," I pointed. "He's asleep."

"I am *not*," came a voice from the sleeping bag.

"You looked like you were asleep."

"Well, I'm not. I'm not some little kid that has to go to sleep this early."

"That's right," said Cally. "He's not little Dilly any more. He's *big Peter* who stays up all night and never goes to sleep."

"Shut your face, Cally."

We were good friends all right. Only good friends could talk to each other like that, and still pal around, day after day. Or, maybe the real truth was that we really didn't know many other kids, at least, none who had BB guns. Cally and I leaned back on our elbows and watched the smoke from the house fire drift lazily toward the full moon.

I think I was drifting off when Cally said, "I've got one for you. And you have to answer fast, without thinking about it, O.K.?"

"So this is a riddle?"

"Ya."

"O.K."

"Answer fast now." I could see his teeth in the dark and I knew he was smiling. "Where do you go to get a newspaper? Quick! Quick!"

"Easy," I laughed. "Blind Billy's News Stand."

"Where?"

"You heard me, Blind... oh..."

"So, how come they call him Blind Billy?"

"Well, because he is..."

"So's the Chinaman... not blind... but you know... you can tell what some people are just by looking at them," said Cally. "What's Blind Billy's real name, anyway?"

"Billy."

"Real smart, Fester. His *last* name."

"I don't know."

"His store isn't even called Blind Billy's. It's R.R. News and Tobacco."

"Nobody calls it that," I had to admit. Everyone I knew, even my dad calls it Blind Billy's. And come to think of it, I had never heard my mom complain when he did. Cally must have been reading my mind.

"You oughta try that one on your old lady."

"O.K.," came the voice from Peter's sleeping bag. "I've got

a question I've always wondered about."

"What? How to get to school?" smirked Cally. "Easy, you just wait till someone calls on you and you follow them over."

"No. Not that!"

"What then? I can hardly wait. Oh, please tell us, big Pete, what is your mind-boggling question?"

"Why do they call them Dixie Cups. What's a Dixie, anyway?"

"Who cares?" retorted Cally.

"I just would like to know, that's all," said Peter. "I'd also like to know who makes the spoons for the Dixie Cups."

"What?!" Cally and I laughed. We had said it together.

"Who cuts them out. They're made of wood, right? Somebody has to cut them out."

"Oh, man," said Cally.

"Do you know how hard it must be to get the wood that thin so they can cut them out?" asked Peter. "And they never have slivers. They're always perfectly smooth."

"Maybe they make them in the back room of the Chinaman's." suggested Cally. "They have to make chopsticks all thin and smooth. Maybe it's the same thing."

That remark tweaked my memory and I reached into my rucksack for my package of grape Jell-O. We always stopped at Fong's for supplies before heading out on a long bike ride. I liked some Jell-O powder to suck on. Just a little on your tongue was quite a sensation. Dilly preferred peanuts. He would buy a bottle of pop and drink it down a couple of inches and then pour the peanuts in. That way he could steer his bike with one hand while having pop and peanuts with the other.

Who made the Dixie Cup spoons would be added to the list of mysteries in our young lives, like who stole the food. On our last scout camp, our Scoutmaster had told us we'd be tested for a couple of badges. We'd have to know how to follow tracks and we'd have to be very good with Morse Code. We got to the campsite down by the river just as the sun was setting. We had to get our tents up before it was too dark to pound in the pegs. I was also hoping to get my cooking badge, so it was my responsibility to get up early and get a fire going and cook the bacon and eggs. Scoutmaster Hunter would be watching to see how quickly I could get a fire started and what kind of a cook I was.

He was a demanding leader. At the last troop meeting, he suddenly told Cally to lie down on the ground and start screaming, and then he told Danny Whitley, who had just gotten his first aid badge, to calm Cally down and get a splint on his broken leg. He told Cally to keep hollering. Poor Danny couldn't remember what to do and Hunter made him rip the first-aid badge off his shirt right on the spot. He told him that when you wear a badge, it means you're qualified. Danny's parents showed up the next week and demanded Hunter be kicked out as Scoutmaster, but the rest of us shouted them down. We thought he was cool. So did Danny. He stayed and earned his badge back.

Now it was going to be my turn. I climbed out of my tent and checked the food one more time to make sure everything was there. Bacon, eggs, butter, and some pancake mix. I turned around to stack the kindling for the fire. Everything was ready. I took one last look. Oh, nooooo. The food was gone!

I knew exactly where I had put it a minute before and it was gone! I started walking around in a panic, wondering where it was and who could have moved it and why – but it was nowhere to be found.

"All ready for the morning, Lester?" Scoutmaster Hunter called from his tent.

"Uh, the food is gone."

"What do you mean, gone?"

"It was here a minute ago and now it's gone. What should I do?"

"That's not my problem. You were supposed to make sure everything was ready."

"I did. I checked it a couple of times. It's gone!"

Now the others were coming out of their tents and there

was quite a commotion when they discovered there was no food. "What are we supposed to do?" they asked the Scoutmaster, peering through the now dimming light.

He seemed strangely disinterested. "Well, I don't know," he said. "We came out here to get a cooking badge and a tracking badge and a Morse Code badge, so where does that leave us?" He got into his pick-up and drove away. We saw the truck lights go over the bridge and then disappear on the other side. We wondered where he was taking off to. Maybe to get more food?

We looked helplessly at each other. The boys shined their flashlights around the camp. There was no food to be found.

"Hey!" someone shouted. "Look at this! A twig on this bush is tied in a knot. And over there – some stones are arranged to point that way!" We recognized it from the tracking class. Flashlights converged on the spot.

Then it came to us: this was the *test*. We walked carefully through the dark; following the signs as we went. They soon ended at the edge of the river and we stood there wondering what to do next.

Then we saw it. Across the river. A flashing light. Someone with a huge flashlight was flicking it on and off. It was Morse Code.

We did find the food. And, after passing our tests, it sure tasted good. When he was asked after breakfast who had taken the food, Hunter would only smile.

We talked about that as we laid there smelling the smoldering cabin. Then our comments got further and further apart until no one talked at all.

CHAPTER EIGHT

I**T WAS SOME KIND OF** an insect that buzzed across my face and woke me up. Sunlight was filtering through the trees. I lay there for a moment, thinking about all that had happened the night before. I turned over and gazed at the house. It looked pretty ugly. It smelled even worse. I looked at Dilly. He was still sleeping, but he was stirring, so I knew he was all right. Cally was still asleep.

And then I spotted it, at the end of my bedroll. "Oh, no!" I said, right out loud.

Cally woke up. "What's the matter?" I held up the empty pickle jar. "I guess we fell asleep," said Cally, rubbing the sand out of his eyes. "We didn't get the headless woman."

I screwed the top off, peeked through the air holes at Cally, and then tapped it against the bottle a few times, thinking. Then I screwed it back on again.

"Sorry, man. You think your dad will be mad?" asked Cally.

"Maybe it's not too late. I could hurry down to the cave right now. I know exactly where it is, and I could probably make it down there and back, and still get into town. Sure. There's lots of time. He doesn't need it till about ten o'clock. That's still hours away."

"It's going to be pretty tough," said Cally. "We were supposed to get one last night. That was the plan."

I sat down and put my head in my hands. "My dad is going to be so disappointed," I said. "I didn't want to let him down."

"Nothing you can do, Fester."

"*Lester*," I said.

"Oh, not you *too*, man!"

"We shouldn't have come in here," I said. "We were given a job and we blew it. If we'd gone where we were supposed to, we'd have the headless woman, instead of an almost headless Dilly."

"Don't you mean *Peter*?" Cally chided.

"O.K., so it takes some getting used to."

Cally reached into his backpack and brought out a roll of toilet paper. "I'm going for a walk," he said, disappearing into the trees.

Dilly woke up and looked around. "Where's Cally?" he asked.

"Back in the bushes."

"Oh." He nodded.

I sat staring at the ground, trying to decide what to do next. There had to be a way to make this happen.

At first it sounded like an animal coming through the brush. It was moving quickly. Then we could hear Cally hollering, "Fester, Fester!"

"Maybe coyotes are after him," said Peter, picking up his gun and levering a BB into the chamber. Despite our earlier discussion about the effectiveness of BBs against wild animals, for some reason I did the same.

Cally burst through the bushes and landed beside us. "They're out there! They're... out... there!" he panted, trying to catch his breath. "In an old shed." He was standing up now, pointing. "I went in and there were a whole bunch of them in the rafters. Bring your pickle jar and follow me!"

It was the scariest thing I had ever seen. The bats were hanging from the low rafters of a falling-down shed. There were maybe five or six. I looked at Cally in the dim light. I think we were both shaking. Cally wanted to catch one since he saw them first. Holding his trembling hand as steady as he could, he carefully extended the pickle jar and slipped it up over the nearest one. Afraid it would somehow get free, I reached over and slammed the bottom of the jar so the top would hit hard against the rafter, making sure the bat was trapped inside. The bat let go, fell down into the jar and I quickly reached in and snapped the lid on. The other bats went wild, suddenly spread their wings and flew around us and then outside. The bat in the jar was struggling. At least Dad had put holes in the lid so the bat could breathe.

When we got back to the campsite a few minutes later, Dilly - make that Peter - had everyone's bed roll tied up and everything back in our packs.

"Let me see. Let me see!" he said. "I've never seen one up close before."

"Neither has anyone else," I said, hoping my voice was not quavering. "Dad says that's the whole trick. When you go into the tent to see the headless woman, they don't let you get very close to *her*, either."

WE BIKED PAST Peter's house but he didn't want to go in. "I want to see what your dad has to say when you give it to him," he said.

"He might not be up yet - it's still early."

"He'll get up for this," said Cally.

As we turned into the driveway, we could see my dad in the garage. He was up already, painting something. He turned and said, "Did you get it?" I held up the jar and he took it from my hand. He examined the prize carefully and said, "This is a beauty. You boys did a good job. Have any trouble getting it?"

"No," I said. "There was nothing to it."

"How was the camping?"

"Oh, you know, the usual," I lied.

"Well, thanks, guys. You've still got a couple of hours to grab some shut-eye. I know you've probably been up talking all night. And you'll want to change your clothes. You smell all smoky. You must have had a good fire."

Cally looked at the ground and grinned. Peter had been standing with his bike behind Cally as much as possible, but Dad finally spotted him and said, "What happened to you?"

"Sort of fell off my bike. Hit my head on a rock."

"You boys made a pretty good bandage there. I told you that first aid course they made you take in Scouts would come in handy. You'll want to let the doctor have a look at that right away, though; make sure there's no infection or anything."

"Yeah. I will," said Peter, turning his bike down the driveway.

"So, what is that you're painting, Mr. West?" asked Cally.

"It's a backdrop for the bally stand, the stage. How does it look?"

"Scary. Just like the big posters outside the tent with the headless woman. Is that blood on the fangs?"

"That's right. Show time will be at about eleven if you want to be there."

Cally turned his bike down the driveway. "I'll call you later," he shouted over his shoulder.

CHAPTER NINE

THE JANZ BOYS HAD BUILT a nice little stage in front of the church tent. It even had a tall frame at the back. Dad had asked them to build it that way so he could tack up a big poster. It was made of a huge sheet of cardboard, and I was holding it up while Dad did the nailing.

"That is just terrible," came a disgusted voice from behind us. I turned around to see Mrs. Johnson. "That thing does not belong in front of a church booth! Just wait till the Reverend gets here."

"The Reverend *is* here," he said, coming up behind her.

"Explain just what exactly Hal is doing on this... this... stage," she demanded.

"He's doing the Lord's work, Mrs. Johnson; helping us raise the funds we need."

"Look at that thing!" she protested. "It looks like a poster of the devil himself. It looks black and evil, and look at the little horns...."

"Those are supposed to be ears," said my dad.

"And those fangs. Is that supposed to be blood? I do believe I'm going to be ill."

Other members were crowding around now, and the Reverend suggested they take Mrs. Johnson into the shade of the tent, and let her sit down. There were many quizzical looks and unspoken questions, but the Reverend told them everything was in order, and it might be a good idea to get some burgers and weiners on the grill.

"We'll start the show in about fifteen minutes," said Dad. "People should be arriving on the midway about then. Oh, here comes Jed. Did you bring it?"

Jed Wellenby held up a small aquarium with a couple of little tree branches in it.

"Did you get a curtain of some kind, too?"

"Got everything you asked for," replied Jed with a big smile.

Everybody followed Dad and Jed to the back of the tent. "It's important we have this display at the very back," explained Dad. "Put the aquarium on that little table, and get that thin piece of wood to cover the top ready. I'm just going to transfer our little headless woman into the glass cage. There - in she goes. Get the top on - we don't want to lose her now. That's it. Now drape the curtain around so it makes a nice display." Dad stood back. "What do you think?"

"You think *that's* going to sell hamburgers?" asked Mrs. Gillespie. "It would put me off my food if I had to look at it."

"Hamburger. Nice touch, Mrs. Gillespie," said Dad. "Get me a chunk of raw hamburger. We'll toss it in the bottom for effect." He looked around the tent. No one seemed particularly impressed with this display. "Who's going to be at the front?" asked Dad.

"Mary and I will," answered Mrs. Janz through tightened lips.

"Make sure as the people file in, they pay their money on the far side; and escort them down that side of the tent to the display."

"But," said Mrs. Janz, "the food is on the other side of the tent. Why would they pay here, before they even know what they want to order?"

Reverend Schmidtke was grinning from ear to ear. "Hal, you old dog, you. This is going to be like running your pick-up truck in reverse in a circle to get where you are going, isn't it?"

"What does that mean?" someone asked.

"It's kind of like the locals fooling each other, instead of letting the carnies have all the fun," answered the Reverend. "I haven't seen this scam run for years."

"Someday, we've got to have a chat, Reverend," said my dad, slyly.

"Yes, *someday*. Just let me handle things at this end, Hal. I know exactly what you need. Okay, people. Listen. We're going to move all the chairs and tables *that* way - got it?" he motioned. "*That* way. I want an aisle down *that* side, to keep the people going in one direction in case this place gets overcrowded. Let's do it!"

I saw Cally come into the tent. "We've got a few minutes, Cally. Want to walk down the midway?"

"Sure. I called but you had already gone."

"Had to help my dad nail up the poster. Looks pretty good, doesn't it?"

"Yeah. Not bad."

We were headed for the booth that had the BB guns. Three shots for a nickel. Break a balloon. Win a prize. Cally plunked down his nickel and squeezed off a shot. *Pap*. No balloon broke. "I was dead on," he said. "I don't see how that one could have missed." He levered the gun and took careful aim. *Pap*. Nothing. "What's going on here?" he said, suspiciously.

The man in the booth said, "It's all in the way you plant your feet, boy; it's all in the position. All in the stance. Sometimes, even the way you hold your mouth can make a difference. Try again. You've got a shot left." *Pap*. Nothing.

"I think the sights are off," said Cally.

"How about you?" said the carnie, motioning to me. I put down my nickel and squeezed one off. *Pap*. Nothing.

"Where did you aim?" asked Cally.

"Dead center on the blue one."

"I saw where it hit the wall. That gun shoots low and to the left."

I took aim. *Pap.* "They've jiggered these guns somehow," said Cally. "At this distance, if one of our guns had hit the wall, the BB would just about have come back in your face. That last one you shot just dribbled off the wall. These guns have no power. The BB starts falling the second it leaves the barrel."

"I suppose they could be getting old," said the carnie.

"How about letting us bring our own guns?" I asked.

"Nope. Can't do it. Regulations. All the guns have to be on chains, just like these, so no one gets hurt."

Pap. I squeezed off my last shot. Nothing. I threw the gun down on the counter.

"Looks like there's something happening down around your church tent," said Cally.

"Is Dil... uh... Peter coming down?"

"No, he called. His head is really hurting. He's staying home in bed. Says it doesn't hurt as bad when he lays down."

"He must have been hurt worse than he let on."

There was a small crowd around the stage. My dad was up on it wearing some kind of a cape I'd never seen before. "It's right here, folks!" he announced. "Some call it the eighth wonder of the world. It's as small as your fist," he said holding his fist in the air, "but as deadly as a charging elephant, and we've got the only one in captivity. The time is now, the place is here. Step right up and have a close look…at a *deadly vampire bat!*"

The crowd didn't move. Some people smiled to themselves, and looked knowingly at their friends. They knew my dad as a truck driver, not someone who would be doing something like this. Others wandered a short distance away, so they'd appear not to be all that interested, when really they were still curious and kept watching.

"Is it stuffed like the toy animals at the booths?" someone shouted.

"No sir, this vampire bat is alive. Alive and hungry for its next victim. We've got someone in there right now, feeding it raw hamburger to keep it from getting violent."

"How do we know it's a vampire bat?" someone else shouted.

"Look at the poster," motioned Dad. "See the blood dripping from its fangs...?"

"That's just a picture!" came the snarly response.

"What do you think we used for a model?" asked Dad. "All right, folks, the place is here and the time is now. Step right up and have a look at the vampire bat that very nearly killed a man right here in Rascal River last night! It took a special vampire patrol to catch it and bring it in alive! Twenty-five cents! Two-bits to see the killer vampire bat. Who'll be first? Who among you is not afraid to look death in the eye?"

"So, who did it nearly kill?" came a shout from the crowd.

Dad waved at a carnival trailer parked just off to the side of the midway. "You're going to meet him right now. He's just coming out of that trailer. Just getting up from what could have been his death-bed. Now, as he makes his way over here, I'm going to ask you folks to do something for me. I want you to move forward. Everybody, please move forward. We don't want to obstruct the other booths. Let's make room for the other people coming this way. Everybody move forward, please. That's it. Besides, there will be a special price of admission for the people at the very front, and something for free as well!"

"Yeah, what?" came the cry.

"You'll have to be up close to the front to find out, sir. I'll only be making the special offer to the people at the very front."

As people started to crowd in, Reverend Schmidtke said to the people at the grill, "Onions. Loads of onions. Just put piles of onions on that grill."

"We've already got enough cooked onions. If we make more, we'll end up throwing them out," somebody argued.

"What you don't realize," said the Reverend, "is that Hal is out there selling the sizzle, not the burgers, and we're going to do the same thing." He took a huge pot of chopped onions and poured it on the grill. The aroma wafted out over the crowd, and people close to the front of the tent started buying burgers.

"Hey, it's working," said Mrs. Johnson, gleefully.

"Not yet, it's not," said the Reverend. "If those folks knew anything about the carnival, they'd know these burgers will soon be free. Or at least, they'd look like they were free," he chuckled.

"What?"

"Wait and see," said the Reverend, grinning widely, "wait and see. The magic is about to happen. I can feel it!"

"Make way, folks," said Dad. "Make way for the vampire victim." The young man climbed up on stage. He wore jeans and no shirt, and his right shoulder had a heavy bandage on it.

"This innocent young man, a visitor to our fair town, was out for a delightful stroll late last evening taking in some night air. About midnight, under the light of the full moon, he was viciously attacked by a creature so black it fairly blended in with the night. Had we not heard his screams and run to his rescue, the blood would have been sucked from his very body."

There was chatter through the crowd. "I'm going to ask this brave young man, if he can, without reliving the horror of his near death, to peel back the bandage, and show you the marks of the fangs that went deep into his body, thirsty for blood." The young man slowly peeled back the bandages, and leaned forward to show his wounds. An old farmer in bib overalls standing near the front shouted, "Hey, that ain't nothin' but a snake bite. I've seen lots of 'em."

"What's your name, sir?" asked Dad.

"Henry Turnbull, if it's any of your dang business..."

"You're not THE Henry Turnbull?"

"I don't know what you mean, hah hah." He was looking at his feet now, a little self-conscious.

"I've heard talk about a Henry Turnbull at the barber shop. Folks say nobody knows more about snakes than Henry Turnbull. Is that right?"

"Well, I don't know. I guess I've dealt with my share of snakes over the years."

"Henry, these people need to meet a man of your

qualifications. I'm going to ask you to come up on the stage."

"No, I don't... uh..."

"Go on, Henry," somebody shouted. "We want to know if this guy is pulling our leg." He shook his head and waved Dad away with a big farmer hand. "Come on, Henry," people shouted. A couple of guys helped him up on stage, and Dad shook his hand and tried to make him feel at ease.

"Now, I realize, Henry, that from where you were standing this could look like a snake bite; but I want you to take a close look, now. Take a *real* close look. Do those marks look like they came from a snake, or aren't they just a *little* bit too close together? What do you think, Henry?"

"That wound is pretty swollen up. Could be they are a little close. I don't know."

"Let me ask you this, Henry: how many snake bites have you seen over the years?"

"Oh, I don't know. Maybe... uh... twenty-five or thirty."

"And where do snakes strike, Henry?"

"Oh, usually the ankle or the leg."

"Why is that, Henry?"

"Well, that's only how far up they can strike."

"You ever seen a snake jump six feet in the air to strike a man in the shoulder, Henry?"

"No."

"You still think this man was snake bit?"

"Maybe he was down close to the ground."

"You mean maybe he was crawling down the street on all fours?" Dad bent over at the waist and moved his arms so he looked the way dogs do when they swim across a creek. Dad laughed and the crowd picked it up and laughed with him.

"Henry, where do we find snakes around here?"

"Down by the river. Anybody knows that."

"How about here in town?"

"Nope. Not a chance. In forty years I've never heard tell of a snake in town."

"Well, you're the expert. Henry, if I asked you to take off your boots right now, and walk across that field over there, would you be afraid of getting snake bit?"

"There are no snakes out there," he said, positively.

"Folks," said Dad, putting his arm around the young man's shoulder, being careful not to touch his wound, "this man was bitten at midnight, just three blocks from here, under the full moon, on the shoulder. Does anybody here still think it was a snake bite?"

"How do we know he wasn't down at the river?" asked Henry.

Dad pulled a paper from his pocket, unfolded it, and held it in the air. The crowd was silent. "This is a hospital report, signed by Doctor Campbell. Do you know Doctor Campbell, Henry?"

"Of course I know him - he just delivered my first grandson. Last week," he smiled.

"All right!" shouted Dad, "Henry's first grandson, let's hear it for him!" Everybody applauded. Some hooted. Others whistled through their teeth.

Inside the tent, the Reverend said, "He's good. He's got that crowd warm now. They're finally coming over to his side. He'll throw them the sucker bait any minute."

"I want you to examine this document, Henry. It says this man was bitten right over there on Fourth Street." Henry took the paper and studied it.

"Henry," said Dad. "Do snakes fly?"

"NO," he laughed. "Of course not."

"You're sure about that? We don't want to trick anybody here, do we, Henry?"

He shook his head.

"Snakes don't fly?"

"Nope."

"Anybody here disagree with Henry? Anybody here that's ever seen a snake fly, put up your hand. Nobody? Then, Henry, let me ask you this - and I'm asking you as a recognized expert: what was it that came out of the full moon, and attacked this man, and bit him on the shoulder!?" Dad grabbed Henry's shoulder sharply as he said it, and Henry blurted out, "I guess it could have been a bat!"

"Thank you, Henry. Now folks, you've been standing here for quite a while in the sun, and you've given us your attention, and I want you to know how much I appreciate that. And - oh look," Dad held up his wrist and tapped on his watch. "It's twelve o'clock and I know you're mighty hungry..."

"Slick," said the Reverend. "Here it comes..."

"And I know," continued Dad, "that there are still some unbelievers in the crowd. So, I'll tell you what I'm going to do. You ten folks along the front of the stage... you, and you... three, four, five six, seven, eight, nine, ten. I want you folks to step into the tent, at no charge. Go ahead. Go right down to the back and see what's there. Go ahead. You holler out to us what you find."

The crowd waited, then: "It's in here all right!" a couple of people shouted. "It's alive! Ooooo - it moved! It looked at me! Ewwwww!"

"What's in there?" shouted Dad into the tent.

"A vampire bat!" someone shouted back, excitedly.

The crowd began to surge forward. "Since it's been exactly twelve hours since the attack, folks," said Dad, "I'm going to make you a special offer, because I don't want anybody on this entire midway to miss out seeing this creature. Here's what I'm going to do. You pay the man at the gate a two-bits to go down and see the killer vampire bat. After you've seen it, after you've looked into its vicious little eyes, and walked away alive to tell about it, if you think you can still bear to stomach some food, we will give you, absolutely *free* - yes, you heard me right, I said *free* - your choice of a hamburger or a hot dog and pop, and... *and...* a free Dixie Cup. Folks, if you think there's a better deal on the midway, then run from here now, as fast as your legs can carry you, and go there! The time is now, folks! The place is here! The line forms on the right!"

It did.

© Eric Kitiyama/Dreamstime.com

CHAPTER TEN

IT WAS NOW THREE IN the afternoon, and the line-up to see the bat had not slowed down. Word had spread all over the midway about the vampire bat and the free food. Only for those who could still eat after looking at the bat, of course. Dad was still on the bally stand, but about all he was doing was directing people in.

"If I'd known the bat was a killer, I wouldn't have used my bare hands," snickered Cally.

"You just slipped the jar over her while she was sleeping," I reminded him.

"It was still my bare hands on the jar."

"Oh, bo-o-oys," cooed Mrs. Johnson, "I want you to meet my nieces. They're from the city, in the same grade as you I think, and I told them how you were the brave boys who captured the bat. Judy and Tamara, this is Lester and..."

"Calvin," said Cally. "My name is Calvin. Pleased to meet you."

"Excuse me for interrupting," said the Reverend. "Boys, Sheriff Roberts wants a word with you. He didn't want to make you feel funny by coming in to get you, but he's waiting out behind the tent in his patrol car."

We went outside and peered cautiously around the side of the tent. He waved us over, and pushed open the door. "Get in," he smiled. "So, which one is Cally?"

"Calvin, my name is Calvin."

I looked him square in the face and silently mouthed, "Cal-vin? Cal-vin? Cal-vin?"

He mouthed back, "Suck rocks!"

"Good shooting, Calvin," said the sheriff.

"Uh... thanks."

"Doc Campbell told me what happened. We found that pick-up and the preacher was actually driving it around town when we pulled him over. He pretty much had to admit he was involved in that fire."

"Why was he even out there?" I asked.

"I asked him that," answered the sheriff. "Turns out a couple of boys who'd had too much to drink stumbled into his tent thinking it was a circus or something and demanded to see the lions and tigers. When he explained why the tent was there, I guess they mocked him and said some nasty things. He gave them some mumbo-jumbo about people spending their money on spirits instead of spirituality. Funny thing was, I almost thought I could smell liquor on *his* breath. Anyway, he says one of them took a swing at him and then they took off, driving down the road. He was mad and jumped in his truck and chased them to teach them a lesson or something..."

"He didn't actually *start* the fire," said Calvin.

"The intent seemed to be there; that's all that matters to the law," explained the sheriff.

"So is he in jail?" I asked.

"No, he's gone. They got that tent down in jig time and got out of here."

"How come you let him go?" asked Calvin.

"That's just the way things work out, sometimes."

"What do you mean?"

"Well, you see, the cabin those moonshiners had broken into and were using once belonged to Rudy Gertsma. He died some years ago, and his son, Ted, inherited the place, but he lives in town. Didn't keep it up or anything. He was planning to sell it. When I told him how it had burned down and how there'd be a trial and everything, he said he just didn't have time, because he's leaving for Europe soon. Going to be gone for a few months. He said if the preacher would just pay for the cabin to be re-built, he wouldn't lay any charges."

"So the preacher paid?" asked Calvin.

"Oh-h-h-h yes, you bet. You should have seen the trunk full of money that preacher had. I knew they made good bucks but I didn't know how much. Ted gave him a figure, which may have been a little high, but the guy didn't argue for a minute. He just wanted to pay up and get out of town. Ted sends his thanks and he asked me to give you boys this, to split among yourselves."

It was five ten dollar bills. "Whoooooee!" whooped Calvin. "We're rich."

"I guess you weren't at home for that bit of excitement around your place last night, Lester," said the sheriff.

"What excitement?"

"When Charlie Murdock nailed the carnie who was stealing gas."

"No, I didn't hear about that."

"Your dad actually took him to the hospital."

"Yeah? What happened? Murdock beat the guy up?"

"No, someone had stolen the gas out of Murdock's truck the night before and he'd been in to see me, but with the rodeo in town and all, I told him there wasn't much I could do. I was too busy. Well, Murdock slams out of the office saying if I can't catch a gasoline thief, he can."

"So, how did he do it?" asked Calvin.

"You have to understand that what he did was against the law, but the guy that got caught doesn't want to lay any charges, so that's that."

"What did he do, Sheriff?" I asked.

"I don't want you boys to ever try this."

"No, we won't."

"It is pretty ingenious when you stop to think about it," he chuckled. "I don't know how Murdock's mind works. He goes down to the river, and catches himself a rattlesnake. He's about the only guy I know who is not afraid of snakes. He brings it home and ties it around the middle with a length of binder-twine, and then ties the other end around the drive shaft of his truck. Well, I guess the snake fights it for a while, till he's good and mad, and then he crawls under the truck and maybe lies in wait. Murdock goes down to the midway. While he's gone, along comes this carnie to steal the gas out of his truck, and the snake gets him."

"How do you know he was stealing gas? Maybe he was just passing by," said Calvin.

"Well, the chunk of garden hose was still hanging out of the gas filler, and there was a gas can lying there with the carnival's name right on it. Besides, he finally admitted it."

"Wow," said Calvin.

"He'd be in jail right now, Lester, if it wasn't for your dad. He is a fine Christian gentleman, and I want you to know that."

"What did he do?" I asked.

"Well, not only did he get this man to the hospital, but I happened to be there on another matter, and when I figured out what happened I was just about to cuff the guy, when your dad steps in. He'd been waiting around to see if the guy needed any help or anything, and when he hears how the guy got bit, he says he's got an idea. He says if Murdock doesn't want to press charges... and he didn't think Murdock would..."

"Why not?" I asked.

"Because then the whole story would come out, see, and Murdock would have to be arrested for the snake thing. You can't lay a trap like that. It could kill somebody."

"Yeah, I guess you're right."

"So, your dad says this guy shouldn't get off scot-free, and I agree, but I say, what can we do about it? Your dad says, 'Don't tell him he won't be charged, just tell him that in this town we let people who steal gas pay their debt to society by working around the town'. I ask him what he's getting at, and he says to tell the guy he can either spend two weeks cutting weeds, or two days working in our church kitchen."

"Oh-h-h-h," I said.

"Your dad said he figured it would be good for him to be around some honest church people, and see what an honest day's work was all about, and I agreed."

"Uh huh," I said, watching Calvin, who was trying not to laugh.

"So what did they have him doing?" asked the Sheriff. "Did they have him flipping burgers or selling them... or...?"

"I guess you could say he was selling them," I answered.

"Good. Good. I just wanted to make sure he showed up. The guy is lucky to be walking around, you know. He'd be a mighty sick man, or maybe even dead, if it wasn't for George Fong."

"What do you mean?" I asked.

"Didn't your dad tell you?"

"He's been pretty busy..."

"Well, he was helping the carnie walk down to the hospital, holding him up, and the guy's carrying on something awful. Sweating. Says he wants to vomit. He thinks he's going to die. They're walking past Fong's store and the light comes on in the room above it, and George sticks his head out the window to see what's going on. Your dad hollers up that the guy's been snake bit and the doctor's away but he's getting him to the hospital anyway. George comes down and says the guy shouldn't be walking and they lay him on the sidewalk under the streetlight and George has something he uses to clean the bite, some kind of liquid stuff. I don't know what it was, but the folks at the hospital say it maybe saved the guy's life. Then somebody in a pick-up stopped to see what was happening, and they laid him in the back and got him that last few blocks to the hospital."

"Wow," I said. "Mr. Fong saved a man's life – I wonder how he knew what to do?"

"He's got some kind of military background. I don't know exactly what it is. During the war he fought for us and spent some time in a jungle somewhere, at least, that's what I heard. So maybe that's where he learned about snakes, I don't know. And not only that, he brings in some kind of medicine from China. Maybe he used some of that. There are people who tell me he's got some stuff that can heal up a scraped leg faster than anything the hospital has. Anyway… you boys could learn a lot about survival from George, especially how to make it when you're all by yourself."

"You mean in the jungle?" asked Cally.

"Or right here, I suppose," said the sheriff. "His wife is still back in China. He's pretty lonely. He doesn't know how long it'll be till he's got the money to bring her here."

Cally looked like he was going to be sick. There was one of his clowning incidents we had never told anyone about. We didn't even talk about it ourselves. It was last Hallowe'en. We'd been out trick or treating. Probably the last year for us, our parents said. They thought we were getting too big for that. We were on the way home, going past Fong's store, when Cally had said, "You know, we should have dressed up like the Chinaman."

He peered into the darkened window of the store. Mr. Fong was likely upstairs in his room. Cally looked at his reflection in the window, framed by the streetlight. In this dark little mirror he put his hands up to the edges of his eyes and pulled the skin back as far as he could. "Welcome to Fong's Fine…." Then he froze. "Oh, no…" he barely whispered.

He was looking into the face of George Fong. He'd been sitting there in the dark, maybe waiting to see if his windows would get soaped. He stared into Cally's eyes for just a moment, then slowly, sadly, lowered his head to his chest.

We ran madly down the street, leaving him there in the dark, all alone. We thought for sure he would tell our parents, but he never did.

* * *   * * *   * * *

YES, THAT HALLOWE'EN was a sad evening for George Fong. He thought, "Another person making fun of how I look. I had sent some clothing home, and they sent me a shirt along with a copy of the Chinese Times. The shirt does have a little different cut, but it keeps me close to my family. The question remains: Can I really bring my wife Lillian here? Or, would we need to move to the city where there is a larger Chinese community, and she can shop every day and enjoy tea and dim sum with new-found friends.

"This was just a child, after all, but maybe this young boy hears things at home that are not kind or maybe it's just the other kids who are not very accepting.

"Will I tell his mother he was mocking me? No. Like the others in my group, I have learned the best way is to be polite, never argumentative in someone else's country. Look for a way to help, and try to be accepted and form relationships in that way.

"At least, this evening I had something to keep me awake. Last night, I felt so lonely. I needed some company but as I went to my friends' restaurant I looked in the front window and they were obviously too busy with customers to talk. Not wanting to walk back home alone, I spent 25 cents and went to a movie. I chose a seat next to the wall, and sat there watching others come in and take their seats. Some had children with them, clutching bags of popcorn. Guys had their arms around their girlfriends. As the theatre began to fill, it seemed very odd that although I was in a room nearly full of people, I still felt lonely. I recognized a few who had come to my store but I don't know if they recognized me; they were more intent on talking with the people they came with. In my mind, I could see how one person to talk with was much more important than a room crowded with strangers who did not communicate with me. For some reason I felt exhausted. I wasn't really following the movie; my mind was in other places, mostly thinking about Lillian.

"Then I was startled by gunfire and all that loud music! Cowboys on horseback were chasing someone across the screen. I had totally lost track of what the movie was even about.

"Then the movie was over and everyone crowded to the exit. It's odd how walking home alone in the dark is even lonelier than walking in the sunshine."

* * * * * * * * *

THE SHERIFF CONTINUED, "You should talk to Eldon Hunter if you're curious about George's background, Lester, he knows him quite well."

"Our Scoutmaster?"

"Yeah. He must have told you how he arranged for George to slip into your camp and carry off your food. Eldon says he was watching from his tent when George walked right by you and you didn't even see him. "

"We didn't know anything about him," said Calvin. And then, "I still don't get something here…"

"What do you mean?" asked the sheriff.

"If you knew the carnie wouldn't be charged, how come you let Lester's dad take him away and use him like that? No offense, sheriff, but this doesn't seem quite right that the sheriff would be involved, and all."

"Ha ha ha," laughed the sheriff. "Truth be known, I owed Hal one. We go back a lot of years, to when the first houses were built on your street, Lester."

"Oh, yeah?"

"When I was building mine - this was before I joined the department, you understand, and we were young and foolish - I was having some trouble with my neighbor. He'd built a retaining wall..."

"What's that?" asked Cally.

"It's a little cement wall just a couple of feet high, so you can make your yard higher than your neighbor's."

"Why would anybody do that?" Cally asked.

"It's so the water runs off your yard when it rains. And it did rain, and the water ran out of his yard and into my basement. I complained, but he refused to talk to me. Said there was nothing I could do about it. I happened to be talking about this at the barber shop, and your dad was there, and he said, 'Why don't you hire a lawyer?'"

"Why didn't you?" I asked.

"No lawyers in this town then. You had to bring one in from the city, and lawyers are often more trouble than... well, never mind. So, anyway, I go home, see, and a little while later your dad shows up. Ha ha. I couldn't believe it. Ha ha!"

"What?" I asked.

"It's the middle of the week, ha ha, and your dad, ha ha, is standing there wearing his 'Sunday go to meetin' suit."

"What's so funny about that?"

"Your dad was working the carnival circuit then, and about the only time he wore that suit was when he got married. This was back in about '46, yeah, not long after the war ended. So, he's standing there on my doorstep wearing this suit, and he's just had his hair cut, and he's got it all slickered down, way too much grease, and I say 'What are you doin', Hal?'"

"And, what was he doing?" I asked.

"He says 'Let's go see your neighbor'. So, we go knock on the door, and the guy answers, and your dad says real stern-like, 'I want to see the retaining wall'. Well, the guy goes around back with us and your dad takes a long look at it, and he looks at the guy, and he looks at the wall, and he looks at the guy again, and the guy is starting to fidget. Your dad looks at me and he says 'We'll sue!'

"The guy goes bananas. He says he didn't know there was a lawyer involved and couldn't we work something out. I start to laugh, I just can't help it. My neighbor asks what I'm laughing at, and your dad says I'm just so happy because when this case is over, I'll own the other guy's house. The guy is in shock. Your dad moves in for the kill. He asks the guy how tomorrow is to go to court, and tells him to bring along the deed to his house. The guy starts to beg. Ha ha ha ha. He says he'll take down the wall, and clean out my basement. Your dad tells him he's got twenty-four hours."

"Did he do it?" asked Cally.

"Yeah, he stayed up all night taking down the wall and hauling away the dirt. Next day he sold his house and I never heard from him again."

"Neat," said Cally.

"I never knew my dad did stuff like that," I said.

"Oh yeah, oh yeah," said the sheriff, wiping his eyes. "Get him to tell you the story of the apple trees some time."

"What apple trees?"

"The ones on the boulevard in front of your house."

"There are no apple trees out there."

"There used to be."

"What happened to them?"

"You'll have to ask your dad."

"Oh, come on..."

"No, I probably shouldn't have told you as much as I did, Lester. You talk to your dad."

"All right."

"Boys, it's been great talking with you, but I've got to go. By the way, I talked with your friend Peter today, and he wanted me to ask you to call as soon as you could."

"Thank you, Sheriff." We got out of the car. "Fifty bucks!" crowed Calvin. "Fifty bucks for one shot! But it's for all of us, so that's like... um... what's three into fifty...?"

"It's only fair," I said. "You made the shot with Peter's rifle."

"I know, and besides we wouldn't have been in position if you hadn't suggested we move Dilly over to the side of the doctor's car."

"Most of that money has to go to your dad, Calvin, for the window."

"Oh yeah, I almost forgot."

We stopped in at Borstad's Hardware and paid Calvin's dad the money, and then stopped off at my place and phoned Peter. "You guys have to get over here, fast! What took you so long to call?" he demanded.

"What's the big hurry?" I said.

"You get over here and find out. This is going to be the best thing you've seen in a long time. And don't come in the front. Come down the alley and in my back door."

"You're not going to tell me what it is?"

"No. Just hurry!"

We did.

CHAPTER ELEVEN

PETER WAS WAITING ANXIOUSLY AT the back door when we arrived. "Come on, come on!" he said. "Hurry!"

We followed him through the kitchen, and then at the entrance to the living room he dropped on all fours. "Get down," he said, "I don't want him to know you're here."

"Who?" asked Calvin.

"You'll see. Just keep down so he doesn't see us at the window."

We crawled over to the picture window, and peered over the sill. "Good thing I stayed home today, or I would never have known," said Peter.

"Incredible," said Calvin. "I had no idea."

Neither had I. We were looking at Tommy Derksen. He was having target practice in his front yard. With a BB gun. Right next door to Martin's place where the window was broken. "How long has he had that gun?" I asked.

"Heck if I know," said Peter. "I just saw him out there with it today."

"Let's go find out," I said, getting to my feet.

We tried to act nonchalant as we walked across the street, but Tommy was still intimidated. He was a year behind us in school, and the sight of the three of us coming toward him had him backing up in his own yard, looking over his shoulder to see how far it was to the front door. We leaned on the picket fence. "Nice gun, Tommy," I said.

"Huh? Oh, yeah... I guess so." He was nervously looking down at it like he was afraid we were going to take it away.

"Had it long?" I asked.

"Got it for my birthday," he replied.

"When was that?" asked Calvin.

"On the seventeenth."

"What date did the window get broken?" Calvin whispered to me.

"I don't know," I whispered back. "Peter?"

He put his mouth to my ear. "I don't know."

"Look, Tommy," I said, "nice talking to you. We'll talk again some time. O.K.?"

"Ya. O.K." He looked greatly relieved as we walked away.

We pored over the calendar on the Brock's kitchen wall. "The seventeenth was a Wednesday," said Peter. "Was that the day Martin did all the hollering?"

"Uh uh," said Cally. "It was the next day. Thursday, the eighteenth."

We went back across the street. "Say, Tommy, we were wondering. With a fine rifle like that," I asked, "how come we never see you out here with it?"

"Well, I ... actually... just used it on my birthday, and then I put it away for a few days."

"How come?" pressed Calvin.

"I don't know. Just got... bored... I guess. Ha ha."

"Or you didn't want anyone to know it was you that broke Martin's window?" asked Peter.

Tommy turned beet red. "Look at him," laughed Calvin. "Have you ever seen a guy who looked so guilty?"

"You must have seen Martin come after us," I said. Tommy made a nervous glance over his shoulder, again judging the distance to the front door.

Calvin caught it. "Don't even think about running, Tommy. We'll pound you right into the ground. You knew Martin blamed us, right?"

"Well, ya... ya... but... um... I just thought you'd... ah... tell him it wasn't you, and that would be the end of it."

"You got any money?" asked Calvin.

"Some."

"How much?"

Tommy reached into his pocket. "Thirty-five cents."

"Thirty-five cents!" exploded Calvin. "We're talking thirty bucks here, that's what the window cost!"

"I've never had that much money," said Tommy. "Anyway, you can't prove I did it, and if anybody says anything, I'll say it wasn't me."

He seemed awfully brave all of a sudden, and the crunch of tires on the gravel on the road behind us soon explained why. His dad had just arrived home.

"Four o'clock," said Tommy smugly. "My dad gets home every day at four o'clock."

"Nice car," said Peter. "New?"

"Got it last year. It's got the double head-lights. We're going in it to Disneyland next summer."

"Lucky you," said Peter.

Tommy's mother came to the door. "Come in and wash up for supper, Tommy." As he hurried across the yard, his dad asked, "You're being careful with that gun, I hope. You know what I told you."

Back in Peter's living room we sat on the couch and stared out the window at Tommy's house.

"I want thirty bucks out of that guy," said Calvin.

"He hasn't got thirty bucks," I reminded him.

"Then I want to take it out of his hide."

"Maybe we should tell our dads and let them handle it," suggested Peter. "Maybe they could get the money out of Mr. Derksen."

"No, we've walked down that road already," I said. "There was a barricade at the end, remember? They didn't believe us."

Silence.

"Well," I said, reflecting on the events of the last couple of days, "we've already paid our money, and we've already looked the killer bat in the eye. You can't get to him because he's in a glass jar, so all that is left is to collect a free hamburger on the way out."

"Whatever are you talking about?" asked Peter.

"Hey, that's right," said Calvin. "He wasn't there. He didn't see your dad's trick with the bat."

"What trick?" asked Peter.

"We'll tell you about it later," I said. "I've got to get home for supper. Can we tent in your back yard tonight, Peter? Maybe we can come up with a plan."

"Sure," said Peter.

"You in?" I asked Calvin.

"I'll be there."

We laid in the tent with the front flap open, looking out at the stars and the full moon. Calvin told Peter what my dad had done with the bat, and we all laughed like crazy. "They cleared over four hundred bucks at our tent," I said. "In one day! Dad says some people came back two or three times and brought other people with them."

"Ya?" said Peter incredulously.

"Ya. My folks came home just as I was leaving. They'd gone down to help take down the tent and everything, and they sold out every bit of food they had. Even had to go get some more! The Reverend said after expenses they still had over two hundred bucks in the kitty."

"How come they call it a kitty?" asked Calvin. "Why don't they call it a puppy?"

"Or a tadpole?" added Peter.

"I've been thinking about what you said this afternoon, Lester," said Calvin, "about us already paying our money, and seeing the killer bat eye to eye, and how we couldn't hurt him because he was protected in a glass jar."

"Ya, so?"

"And you said the only thing left for us to do was get our free hamburger and go home."

"Ya. Some kind of satisfaction. That's all we've got left, now."

"But we were bitten by the killer bat. In this case, Tommy Derksen. He sucked our blood right out of us."

"What blood?" asked Peter.

"The money, stupid, the money!" said Calvin impatiently.

"Oh."

"And," continued Calvin, "you know how you said we couldn't get to the killer bat because it was protected in that glass jar?"

"Yeah."

"Glass breaks."

"Meaning what?"

"Why don't we break the glass and kill the bat?"

"You mean, kill *Tommy*?" breathed Peter.

"That's not exactly what I meant," said Calvin.

"What did you mean, then?" asked Peter.

"I don't know."

"Well, you said it!"

"I *know* I said it. You don't have to tell me what I said!"

We went around and around like that for a couple of hours, and then out of the darkness of our tent came the germ of an idea. It was terrible. It was ugly. It was exciting. It was perfect!

Before sun-up we were back in my garage. My dad had used the side of a refrigerator carton to make his big bat poster. The rest of the cardboard was still in the garage, and we dragged it down the alley and across two blocks of streets to the street Peter lived on.

On one side of the Derksen house was Martin's. On the other side was a vacant lot. We propped the cardboard up along Derksen's fence on the vacant lot side. "You think it'll look like the wind blew it here?" asked Peter.

"The wind doesn't blow stuff this big around," I said.

"Doesn't matter," said Calvin. "I'll bet they don't even notice it's here." We slipped back across the street and into the tent. Waking about nine o'clock, I said, "O.K., synchronize watches. We meet back here at three this afternoon. You sure you can do it, Calvin?"

"Of course I can do it. I'm the guy with the fifty dollar shot, remember?"

"It'll cost a lot more than that if we get caught," I said. "So you have to be sure."

"I'm sure. I'm sure. You just make sure everything else is set up right. Don't worry about me."

* * *   * * *   * * *

THREE IN THE afternoon. We met as planned in Brock's living room, and looked out over the field of battle. He wasn't there. Tommy wasn't outside with his BB gun.

"The whole plan depends on him being out there," moaned Peter.

"We *know* what the plan depends on!" Calvin sounded edgy. "It's your job to make sure he's out there, Lester."

"I'll do it," I said.

"What if he's not home?" asked Peter. "What then?"

"Then we try it tomorrow and the next day, until he is home, or until somebody chickens out."

"I won't chicken out," said Calvin. "I'm not afraid of anything."

We sat there. "If he doesn't come out by three-thirty," I said, "I'll go knock on his door." The minutes ticked by. "Three-thirty," announced Peter, looking at me.

"You better get going, Calvin," I said. He slung his BB gun across his back and went out the back door. We heard him pedal out the back gate. I picked up my gun and walked across the street to Derksen's and knocked on the door. Tommy answered.

"Want to shoot for a while?" I asked.

"How come?"

"Something to do," I shrugged.

"Where are the other guys?"

"Who knows? Gone somewhere I guess. You coming out?"

He looked suspiciously around the yard. "No, I don't think so," he said. "I'm not coming out today."

"Why not?"

"I don't trust you guys. You're probably trying to get me outside so you can jump me."

"Oh, that stuff yesterday? Ha ha. That was... nothing. You see... uh... actually, we're looking for a couple more guys to join our club, but you're the only one we've seen lately with a decent gun."

"What kind of a club?"

"It's a shooting club."

"What's it called?" asked Tommy.

"It's called... um... the... uh... the... the BB Boys. Yeah, the BB Boys. That's what it's called."

"I've got a BB gun."

"Yeah. We saw it."

"Aren't you still mad about the window?" he asked.

"Oh, that? No," I lied, but I could see from the look on his face that he wasn't buying it. I tried something else. "You see, Tommy, it's just that... um... with... with... all the windows we've broken, you know... it was kind of maddening to get nailed for one we didn't do, you know? The other guys are actually laughing about it now. Ha ha ha."

"You've broken other windows?" he asked, eyes wide.

"You have to, to get into the club," I explained. "You see, you've already broken a window, right? So, you've already passed the initiation."

"Do you have to pay any dues, like at Cubs?"

"No, no dues. We don't believe in dues."

I glanced at my watch. Time was getting short. "Of course, there still is one other thing you have to do," I said.

"What's that?"

"You have to prove you can shoot."

"I can shoot."

"You have to be able to knock three cans off the fence in sixty seconds. Can you do that?"

"I don't know. Probably."

"Come on out now, and let's find out."

"I don't know..." Tommy was acting suspicious again, his eyes darting around the yard.

"Well, O.K.," I gambled, "if you don't want to be in the BB Boys, forget it." I turned to go.

"Wait!" he said. "I'll get my gun."

I glanced at Peter's house. He was supposed to be peeking from the front window but I couldn't see him. Tommy came out with his gun. "My dad will be home in a few minutes and I'll have to go in."

"If we don't finish today, we can always try again tomorrow," I said. We fished some blackened cans out of his family's burn barrel, and lined them up on a board we put across a couple of bricks. It was against the fence on the vacant lot side, which also acted as the backstop when the cans went flying. They were about ten feet down from where the cardboard laid against the fence. I fired off about several shots, and so did he. We picked the cans up and started again.

Out of the corner of my eye I caught some movement in the Brock's picture window. The drapes were closing. That was my signal. "Holy Cow," I exclaimed, looking at my watch. "It's nearly four o'clock. I have to get home. See ya!" I dashed out the front gate and across the street. I looked over my shoulder to see Tommy turn back to shooting at the cans, and I deked around the corner of Peter's house and went in the back door.

"You just made it, Lester. Tommy's dad is coming up the street. There was a big truck ahead of him and I nearly missed him."

A moving van rumbled by, and then Tommy's dad braked and turned into the driveway. Tommy turned to salute his dad with his gun, and his dad waved back. Tommy's mother came to the door. "Tommy!"

"Yes, I'll be right there," he said. "Just a couple more shots."

His dad was still half in the car, fishing something out of the back seat. Aiming for a tin can, Tommy squeezed the trigger. *Pap.*

"TOMMEEE!" shouted his dad, still inside the car. "WHAT HAVE YOU DONE?"

Tommy was startled. He wheeled around, and where they had had their backs to each other a second ago, they were now facing each other. Dad with his briefcase, and Tommy with his gun. "You idiot, Tommy!" shouted his dad. "I told you to be careful! Do you know how much this cost?"

Mom was at the front door. "What's the matter?"

"Idiot child here just shot the back window of the Chevy! Look at it!" he roared.

Tommy stared in disbelief. "I did not! I wasn't even shooting in that direction!"

"Look at the back window!" his dad wailed. "I told you to be careful!"

"It wasn't me, honest!"

"Right," said his dad, extending his arm around the yard. "Do you see anybody else here with a BB gun?"

"Well, no... but..." Then Tommy's gaze settled on the cardboard pressed against the fence. "I know what's going on," he shouted, running for the fence.

"Oh, no," squeaked Peter. "We're caught!" We could see Calvin still pressed up against the cardboard, his gun tight against his chest. "They'll see him the minute they look over the fence," said Peter. "I'm going to be sick."

Peter ran to the bathroom, and I felt my heart in my throat as Tommy made it to the fence. He put his hand on the top and was just about to hop over. He would have landed right on Calvin, except his dad grabbed him by the back of the collar and hauled him back. "Don't try to run away from me, you little..." He grabbed Tommy's BB gun out of his hands. Holding it by the barrel, he smashed it on the ground, over and over again. "I should never have bought you this thing!" I'm sure they could hear him all over the neighborhood. Tommy was standing there bawling and trying to point over the fence, but his dad had Tommy by one arm. With his other hand dad angrily threw the BB gun on the ground. It landed inches from Calvin, just on the other side of the fence. Terrified, he hugged the cardboard.

Still holding on to Tommy, his dad reached down and picked up the gun by the barrel and whacked him right across the butt with the flat side of the stock. Tommy yelped. His dad hit him again, and then pointed him toward the house. "Inside! Inside! Inside!" he shouted, punctuating every command with a whack across Tommy's behind.

Tommy's furious father slammed the door behind them, and we waved at Calvin. He had been lying there frantically waiting for the all-clear. Now he jumped up and ran like crazy for the alley behind Derksen's. He climbed on his bike and pedaled madly down the alley to the corner, came across the street and down Brock's alley, and burst in the back door.

"I thought I was dead! I thought I was dead!" he gasped, collapsing on the floor. He could hardly breathe. "They nearly got me! They nearly got me! I have never been so scared in my life! I was scared to death!"

Peter grinned.

"What... are... you... laughing at?" puffed Cally.

"You were scared!"

"Not really scared," defended Cally.

"You said you were scared."

"I didn't mean *scared* scared..."

"What, then?"

"Just sort of... nervous..."

"We saw you run, man. You ran like you were scared!"

"I didn't see you volunteering to make the shot. You were too chicken!" Cally was regaining his composure.

We sat there for a minute, until all of our hearts stopped pounding, and then we cracked the curtains just a bit to view the scene of the crime.

"Look at the window," said Peter. "I thought it was supposed to break."

"It didn't break?" said Calvin. "You mean that was all for nothing?"

"No. Look at it, Calvin. The window is ruined. But it didn't break, it just sort of turned a funny blue color. You can't see through it any more. It'll have to be replaced."

"I wonder if that's what they mean by that new safety glass," said Calvin. "I saw that on T.V. a while ago."

"Can we get away from here for a while?" asked Peter.

"We could go to my place," I offered.

As we biked along, Cally said, "Remember the Alamo!"

We had seen the movie together several years before but we had no idea why he'd bring it up now.

"It's what I was thinking," said Cally.

"What are you talking about?" I asked.

"When I could hear Tommy and his dad getting close to the fence – I thought they would find me and kill me. It was just like being at the Alamo with the soldiers coming – right at the end, you know?"

"Remember the Alamo!" shouted Cally.

"Maybe we should say, 'remember the *blue*,'" suggested Dilly. "It could be our sort of ... secret... code or something..."

As we turned our bikes into the alley, Cally asked, "What is this BB Boys crap?"

"What BB Boys?" asked Peter.

"Lester told Tommy we had a club called the BB Boys.

Where did you come up with a name like that?"

"He asked me the name of the club and I looked down at my gun, and there it was.

"How come you didn't say it was the Three Musketeers?" asked Peter.

"Because then there would have been four, and you can't have four guys in the Three Musketeers. That's why they're called the *Three* Musketeers," lectured Cally.

"It wouldn't have mattered," countered Peter. "We weren't letting him into the club anyway."

As we biked into my driveway, we could smell something yummy. I opened the back door and Mom said, "You're just in time. I've got apple pie just warming in the oven. Bring your friends in and sit down."

"I didn't know you were baking," I said.

Dad came into the kitchen. "She didn't bake these. She bought them at the St. Mary's tent."

"You bought from another church tent?" I asked.

"I felt sorry for them. They had a lot of food left over."

"But weren't they right by the grandstand?" I asked.

"Yes, indeed they were," said Mom. "They drew the best spot this year, and they are not too happy with us, I can tell you. In fact, I'm hearing there's going to be concerns expressed at a special meeting of the ministerial council."

"Here we go again," said Dad. "Accused of being too creative, just like the last time I got called into the principal's office. I remember…"

"Could we leave that story for another time?" asked Mom. She opened the freezer and brought out a container of ice cream. As she cut the steaming apple pies, she put a scoop of ice cream on each, and pushed them over to Calvin and Peter. We were enjoying the pie when Calvin said, "Speaking of apple pies, Mr. West, tell us the story of the apple trees in your boulevard."

"There are no apple trees out there," said Dad, craning his neck to look out the front window in case some had suddenly sprouted.

"Didn't there used to be?" asked Calvin.

"Nope."

"Hmmmm." Calvin raised another forkful of pie to his mouth. Mom put her fork down quickly and it clinked loudly against her plate. Her eyes were questioning.

"Where did you hear about any apple trees?" she asked. Her eyes were narrowing now.

"From the sheriff," said Calvin.

"He shouldn't be telling you boys stories about things that happened a long time ago."

"He told us about the retaining wall,too."

"What retaining wall?" asked Mom. Now it was Dad's turn to put down his fork.

"He told you about the retaining wall?" said dad, breaking into a grin.

"What is this all about?" demanded Mom.

"You didn't know about the retaining wall," said Dad. "I never told you. Ha ha ha ha. I had forgotten all about that until now. Yes, that was Tim Roberts, all right. Ha ha ha."

"Well, tell me," said Mom.

"Forget it. It was a long time ago."

"When we were all building our houses?"

"Yes. So let's just forget it. If we bring all this up again, you'll just get all upset again," said Dad.

"So, there *were* some apple trees?" I persisted.

"Forget it," said Dad. "It was nothing."

"Oh, go ahead and tell them," said Mom. "After the stunt with the bat, it doesn't much matter, does it? "

"Well," started Dad, "by the time we had this house built, the town had poured the cement curbs along the road, and they had the sidewalks in, but the boulevard was a mess. Just this big pile of clay on it, a couple of feet high. We waited for weeks, but they never came around to clear it off so we could plant some grass and your mother... well...," he looked at her.

"Yes. Yes. I know. I nagged you, go ahead and say it. I hated that pile of dirt out there. I wanted some grass and some flowers."

"So," continued Dad, "I had phoned the town office several times and they said they just couldn't get around to grading it. So, then I went down there, and the town engineer, Dan... somebody... who was it?" He leaned back and looked at Mom.

"I know who you mean... he died here a while back... I don't remember his name..."

"Anyway," said Dad, "he gets all upset and says he's sick of hearing from me and as far as he is concerned, the dirt will never get taken away. He says they're going to leave it there all summer, and all winter, and if we're nice, maybe they'll run a grader down there and scrape it off in the spring. And he tells me to get out of his office."

"So, what did you do?" I asked. Calvin and Peter sat entranced.

"Well, I... ah... hah hah hah... I..."

"*I'll* tell you what happened," broke in Mom. "One of his old carnie buddies had shown up and they went downtown and had too much beer."

"Oh, we didn't have that much, Betty; don't tell the boys *that*."

"Oh no? You're telling me that scheme didn't come out of the bottom of a bottle?"

"It worked, didn't it?"

"Are you guys going to tell us?" I pleaded.

"Your father and his drunken friend..."

"He wasn't drunk...," Dad insisted.

"Your father and his *drunken friend*," continued Mom, "went down to the river with a shovel, and dug out three little willow trees. They brought them back here and planted them in that awful pile of dirt out front. I ask them what they're doing that for and they won't tell me. They just go get some more beer, and they end up sleeping out back by the garden."

"Really?" I said. Dad was leaned back in his chair now, staring at the ceiling and smiling.

"The next day," continued Mom, "he brings his friend into the house and the guy gets all cleaned up, and puts on your father's only suit and heads downtown. Again, he won't tell me why this guy is wearing the suit your father got married in."

"And you got all..." started Dad.

"Of course, I got upset. I had a right to get upset! And then, the guy comes back after a while and he and your dad make a bet about how long it's going to take."

"How long what's going to take?" I asked.

"How long it's going to take for the town to show up with a grader and clear the boulevard."

"And I won," smiled Dad. "They showed up first thing the next morning. Woke us up when that grader started moving that dirt. Graded it clean, right down to the sub-soil, put in some good dirt, and even seeded it with grass."

"Yes," said Mom, "and then the engineer comes to the door and says to your father, 'Go ahead - sue me. I'd love to meet you in court!' And then he stomped off out of the yard. And then, your dad and this friend sit down on the floor and laugh until they're just about sick!"

"So," I said, "where do the apple trees come in?"

"There were no apple trees," said Dad patiently. "That's the whole point. Those three willows we planted were... well... *headless women*."

"I'm not getting any of this, Mr. West," said Calvin. "I'm sorry."

"It's because his friend lied," said Mom.

"He didn't exactly lie," corrected Dad.

"Just like you didn't exactly lie about the *killer vampire bat*?" asked Mom.

"All he did," explained Dad, "was go down to the town office and tell the engineer he represented me, which he *did*," he said, looking sideways at Mom. She folded her arms.

"He told them I had just planted some very expensive apple trees in my boulevard, and that if the engineer ordered the boulevard graded anytime soon, he could expect to get his pants sued off."

"He made the engineer think he was a lawyer," said Mom.

"He didn't *make* him think anything," said Dad. "He just let him draw his own conclusions."

"Wow," breathed Peter. "What a neat story!"

"Double wow," said Calvin, not bearing to be outdone.

"By the way," said Dad, "your mom's got some news."

"Yes," she said brightly. "Mr. Fong is going back to China to bring his wife over here. He'll be gone for a few weeks and I'm going to run his store."

"What?" I choked. "How can you do that?"

"I was a check-out girl when I met your dad. I know how to make change, if that's what you're thinking. He had a little sign on the door saying he would be closed in about a week, so I asked him to let me run it and he said O.K."

I just couldn't imagine my mom running a corner store, even if it was just for a few weeks.

"Something else," she said. "I told him there were some elderly people in town who might appreciate a delivery service and he said it would be all right if I hired you to do that on your bike. Unless, of course, you'd still rather pick beans."

"Um, I don't know…"

"And he said if we got busy it would be all right to hire your funny friend as well."

"Which one would that be?" I asked, innocently.

"He said you'd know."

* * * * * * * * *

George Fong had saved almost enough money to bring his wife, Lillian, over from China, but wanting to go back for a visit himself, he sold a share of his store to his friends who ran one of the restaurants, and started packing. As it happened, the restaurant owner was losing some staff and could not run the store completely by himself. He agreed to let mom act as cashier and he would be around regularly to see how things were going.

This was a major step as things improved in George's life. He seldom heard "the Chinaman" anymore, and he was being shown a lot more respect. Still, he would have to decide what would be best for Lillian as she arrived in this new land.

* * *   * * *   * * *

MY DAD LOOKED somehow different to me that day. I thought of him more as a musketeer than a dad. He could have been one of us - if he was younger, of course.

As we sat and mused about the apple trees, Dad said, "Great pie, wasn't it? Don't leave yet, I've got something for you." He dashed out of the house and into the garage. In just a moment he was back, and put the pickle bottle in the center of the table.

"Ooooo," Mom objected. "Did you have to bring that thing in here?"

"Thought you boys might want to release the bat back into the cave," said Dad. "Are you up to it?"

We rode in silence along the pavement out of town, past the site where the big tent had been, and took the downhill grade to the river. We cut off onto the old dirt road and stopped. "This is far enough," I said. "The bat can find its way from here." I twisted off the lid, but the bat didn't fly out. I put the jar down to the grass and gently shook the bat out. It flopped on the ground and then flew into a nearby tree. We got onto our bikes and headed home.

No one brought their BB gun along when we went biking after that. We had never discussed it, but there was just some kind of unspoken feeling that perhaps that part of our lives had left along with the carnival.

I didn't pick beans that summer. I put an extra large basket on my bike, with a little sign that said Fong's Delivery.

A couple of weeks later, Peter called to say his dad had been transferred to a place over a thousand miles away and they were moving immediately. Calvin and I went over to say good-bye.

No one knew exactly what to say. We thought we should say something in parting but no one knew what was appropriate. We had been through so much together. There was certainly nothing I could think of that could possibly sum it all up. After an awkward silence, Cally finally saved the day with, "Remember the *blue*". We repeated it together. Then we shook hands like we had seen men do, and said good-bye.

Calvin's dad asked him to come and work at the lumber yard, pouring nails into bags for the contractors. His dad let him off at four o'clock every day so he could deliver papers for Blind Billy. Calvin stopped by to tell me the man's real name was William Parker. Other than that, Calvin and I didn't see each other much for the rest of the summer.

In the dying days of August, George Fong arrived with his wife, Lillian. He had decided to sell his store completely and move to the city where there was a large Chinese community. He told Mom he thought his wife would be more comfortable there.

In September, Calvin and I walked to school together, as we had done for a few years. After school, he dashed off to the hardware store, and I took over his paper route, and we just gradually drifted apart. It seems like a million years ago now.

CHAPTER TWELVE

ANNE WAS SITTING ON THE edge of the couch, looking down at the rug. Her hands were clasped and she was smiling as she slowly moved her head from side to side.

Jeremy was now lying on the floor, looking up at me. "What a great story, Grandpa!"

"There is a little bit more, Jeremy. Remember when your great-grandfather died and we went back to Rascal River for the funeral?"

"Jeremy was only five," reminded Anne.

"No, I remember," said Jeremy, his eyes lighting up. "We went to that little church..."

"That's right," I said. "While we were there, I had to go down to the town hall to make sure the house was now registered in your great-grandmother's name, and that the property taxes were up to date."

"What are property taxes?" Jeremy asked.

"You have to pay taxes every year for the piece of ground your house sits on, and the house itself."

"Really?" he said. "I didn't know that. Do *we* pay that every year, too?"

"Do we *ever*," answered Anne. "Just one of the many things you have to look forward to." Then, "Was there some problem with the taxes, Dad? You never mentioned any problem."

"No. No problem. Just a very big surprise," I laughed. "In looking over the history of the taxes they'd paid over the last fifty years, I found out that when I was a boy, for a short time, taxes in Rascal River were determined by how far you lived from the geographical center of town: the further you were from the center, the less tax you paid. The closer in, obviously, the *more* you paid. I don't know how they came up with that idea, but apparently it only lasted a couple of years. I asked the clerk where the center of town was back then, and she said it was easy to find because Fong's store was built on it. All those years, George Fong was the center of our little universe and we didn't even know it."

WE WERE QUIET for a moment, thinking about all of this, when Dad continued, "I wonder if Mr. Fong knew he was paying the highest taxes in town. But now I know why the building contractors wanted to know how far the property they were developing was from Fong's store."

"Did you ever see Peter again?" asked Anne, changing the subject.

"No, I'm sorry to say it, but I have no idea whatever became of him."

"What about Calvin? Have you seen him since?"

"He wasn't at the funeral, so afterwards I walked down to where Borstad's Hardware used to be, but it wasn't there any more. It's now a furniture store. I asked around and found out Calvin had actually become the manager of his dad's store, and then they sold out and he and his parents moved down east somewhere. No one is sure exactly where."

"That's too bad," said Anne, quietly.

"Losing a friend is just one of the regrets I have as I get older."

"Regrets?" asked Anne.

"Yes, And, Jeremy, I had to learn over many years what you are learning more about in school and other places these days."

"What's that?"

"To respect other people and their cultures. We have a real diversity in our workplace and it makes us a lot stronger as a team."

"Yes, they mention diversity a lot at school," replied Jeremy.

"We'll talk more later, but if you've got kids in your class who came to this country in search of a better life, you might consider asking them to teach you some of their language. I sure wish I had done that..."

"That might he hard..."

"Yes, but worth it in the long run as you learn to appreciate them and who they are. They may even add something to your life."

Jeremy thought for a moment and then asked "What about your BB gun? Can I see it? Would you let me shoot it?"

"Sorry, Jeremy," I said. "I don't know what ever happened to my BB gun. It just... disappeared... in one of the many moves we made."

"You lost your BB gun?" Jeremy was disappointed.

"It's not as if I *threw* it away, Jeremy," I explained. "It just sort of vanished... along with my youth."

"Bummer," said Jeremy.

"It's my own fault," I said. "It's one thing to lose an old toy. It's quite another to misplace old friends. I guess I should have been at lot more careful. With both."

The End

IF YOU ENJOYED THIS STORY, you might want to check out two of Bob's other books, *Welcome to Radio* and *I'll Puke in Your Pocket*, both available on Amazon.

The Headless Woman
ISBN: 979-8-84291-871-3

blayton@shaw.ca
Front cover by Kylie Kay
Back cover by Rob Hislop.

Daisy Outdoor Products grants Bob Layton permission to use the likeness
and Daisy Trademarked Name in print, specifically for his novella "The
Headless Woman." This permission is not to be construed as endorsement.

Made in the USA
Middletown, DE
13 August 2022

70497096R00066